A SCREENFUL OF SUGAR?

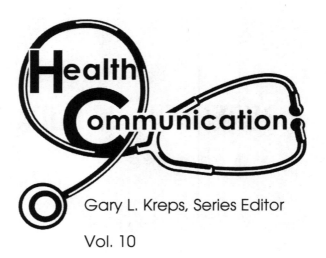

Gary L. Kreps, Series Editor

Vol. 10

The Health Communication series is part of
the Peter Lang Media and Communication list.
Every volume is peer reviewed and meets
the highest quality standards for content and production.

PETER LANG
New York • Washington, D.C./Baltimore • Bern
Frankfurt • Berlin • Brussels • Vienna • Oxford

JON C. SCHOMMER
LEWIS H. GLINERT

A SCREENFUL OF SUGAR?

Prescription Drug Websites Investigated

PETER LANG
New York • Washington, D.C./Baltimore • Bern
Frankfurt • Berlin • Brussels • Vienna • Oxford

Library of Congress Cataloging-in-Publication Data
Schommer, Jon C.
A screenful of sugar?: prescription drug websites investigated /
Jon C. Schommer, Lewis H. Glinert.
pages cm. — (Health communication; vol. 10)
Includes bibliographical references and index.
1. Communication in pharmacy—United States.
2. Pharmacy—Information services—Evaluation.
3. Advertising—Drugs—United States.
4. Telecommunication in medicine—Law and legislation—United States.
I. Glinert, Lewis. II. Title.
RS56.S36   615.1068'8—dc23   2013041249
ISBN 978-1-4331-2509-6 (hardcover)
ISBN 978-1-4331-2508-9 (paperback)
ISBN 978-1-4539-1239-3 (e-book)
ISSN 2153-1277

Bibliographic information published by Die Deutsche Nationalbibliothek.
Die Deutsche Nationalbibliothek lists this publication in the "Deutsche
Nationalbibliografie"; detailed bibliographic data is available
on the Internet at http://dnb.d-nb.de/.

Cover design by Clear Point Designs

The paper in this book meets the guidelines for permanence and durability
of the Committee on Production Guidelines for Book Longevity
of the Council of Library Resources.

© 2014 Peter Lang Publishing, Inc., New York
29 Broadway, 18th floor, New York, NY 10006
www.peterlang.com

Printed in the United States of America

To Lisa and Joan

Table of Contents

Acknowledgments

The authors gratefully acknowledge Daniel Sepulveda Adams, PhD for his assistance in obtaining data about the trends in spending for direct-to-consumer advertising. Dr. Sepulveda Adams is a Research Scientist for PRIME Institute, Minneapolis, Minnesota, USA. The authors also gratefully acknowledge Basma Gomaa, DVM for her assistance in obtaining data about the trends in the use of social media. Dr. Gomaa is a PhD student in Social and Administrative Pharmacy, University of Minnesota, Minneapolis, Minnesota, USA.

Preface

This text is part of a Peter Lang Publishing series in Health Communication. The purpose of the series is to examine the powerful influences of human and mediated communication in delivering care and promoting health. The books in this series describe strategies for addressing major health issues, such as "reducing health disparities, minimizing health risks, responding to health crises, encouraging early detection and care, facilitating informed health decision making, promoting coordination within and across health systems, overcoming health literacy challenges, designing responsive health information technologies, and delivering sensitive end-of-life care."

There has been a global information explosion. A quick trawl on the World Wide Web can land information about anything—including prescription drugs. Information, however, is no prescription for knowledge, let alone for sound decision making. The World Wide Web and the search engines that power it promise the earth, but, as studies consistently confirm, yield large measures of frustration or distraction. With drug information rapidly migrating to the Web, the chronically poor standards of drug information available to consumers in both the developed and the developing world are, in our view, being further compromised—while American marketing of drugs to consumers, hitherto more or less restricted to its own borders, has now been handed a global online audience.

The Internet holds out possibilities for knowledge and decision making across the social and global spectrum that would have seemed a fantasy a generation ago.

It all hangs on the good will and imagination of just a few key players—and the good sense of the ordinary end-user.

Our book offers insight and suggests means for change as we navigate the uncharted waters of prescription drug information and promotion. Amid all there is to analyze and criticize, we have trained our sights on practical outcomes: how can information for consumer decision making be optimized? In our opinion, even manufacturer-sponsored websites can become trusted sources of information since they are scrutinized by the FDA (U.S. Food and Drug Administration) and manufacturers arguably hold the best information available about their products. The challenge is how to make full disclosure of information in a balanced manner and across society.

We first trace the social and political history of prescription drug information and marketing to Western consumers (chapter 1) and in chapter 2 we offer a social and communicative profile of today's prescription drug website and the communicative properties of websites in general. Among our chief concerns: Who uses such drug sites, how and why? How do they compare with more 'traditional' drug information channels? Who is behind drug information and how trustworthy is it? What part do search engines play? What are the hallmarks of user-friendly websites in general? How do text, context, image and message interact in this new hypertextual stew? How are the elderly and less literate faring and what can be done?

Drawing on insights from health education, communication and Web usability, we then describe and evaluate a sample of the most widely used sources of prescription drug information: sites maintained by government organizations (chapter 3), sites maintained by information companies and TV-related sites (chapter 4), health service provider sites (chapter 5), manufacturers' brand sites (chapter 6), and social media, including YouTube and Wikipedia (chapter 7). In each case, the focus is on four dimensions crucial to the success of the message: content, organization, language, and indication of oversight.

In chapter 8, we pull together the lessons of these five chapters in such a way as to offer policy-makers, patient advocates and the health industry a focused and feasible prescription for change. In the last chapter (chapter 9), we come back to you as health-seeker. We provide self-assessment tools that you can use to learn more about yourself and how you tend to use information and make decisions, and how you can avoid the perils of misleading information. We also give pointers on how to evaluate the source of information to see if it is credible and trustworthy. For those who are interested, we provide a self-assessment tool called the Knowledge And Resource Evaluation (KARE) that the patient can complete and then share with a physician and pharmacist to help them understand how the patient likes to receive information and make decisions. Finally, we give pointers about how patients can best utilize the most highly trained and knowledgeable health professional when it comes to prescription medications and how to put all of the diversity of information about them into good decision making. That person is the pharmacist. We explain a new service called Medication Therapy Management that is now covered by most U.S. insurance plans and allows patients to make an appointment with their pharmacist to go over medication-related questions and to discuss how to choose the very best medications.

We hope that this book will be found informative. But more than that, we hope that it will make consumers (for every party to this matter is also a consumer) feel more confident that there are good ways to sort through all of the information about prescription drugs and make the very best decisions for themselves and for their families.

DISCLOSURE

Throughout this book, we refer to names of organizations, companies, products, and services. We do not hold direct financial interest in any of these, but acknowledge that retirement funds in which we have invested are likely to have holdings in some of the companies mentioned in this book. We do not track that, nor do we instruct our retirement fund managers in how to directly invest our funds in such companies.

FAIR USE

In some parts of the book, we include screenshots of information publicly available on the Internet in order for the reader to see examples of information we are discussing. We include these under fair use guidelines in which we reproduce them for purposes such as criticism, comment, reporting, teaching, scholarship and research.

DISCLAIMER

It should be noted that our mention of organizations, companies, products, and services does not represent any endorsement (positive or negative) on our part. We have limited our evaluation and comments to the way information is presented and have used examples for illustrative purposes only. Finally, statements made in the screenshots included in this book should not be used by readers for informational or decision-making purposes. They are part of an information source that is more extensive than what is shown in this book.

CHAPTER ONE

Prescription Drug Information For Consumers

How Did We Get Here?

Over 500 million times a day in the United States, individuals make the decision to take or not to take a prescription medication. Arguably, this decision is the most frequently occurring health care event in society. It far outpaces the 6 million daily visits to the pharmacy (Schondelmeyer, 2009), the 2.6 million daily visits to the physician's office (Centers for Disease Control and Prevention, 2011), the 123,287 daily hospital inpatient procedures, and the 108,041 daily hospital discharges (Centers for Disease Control and Prevention, 2011). The use of medications is probably the only type of treatment we experience on a daily basis. In 80% of cases, chronic diseases are prevented and managed with medications (McGinnis, Strand & Webb, 2010). In any given week, 81% of U.S. adults take at least one medication, and nearly one-third take five or more different medications (Kaufman, Kelly, Rosenberg, Anderson & Mitchell, 2002; *The Chain Pharmacy Industry Profile*, 2001). Over a lifetime, it is estimated that a typical American will take 14,000 pills (Camporesi, 2011). When one considers that a 60-year span of adulthood is about 22,000 days, the frequency with which we interact with medications is astounding.

Taking medicines is not only a frequently occurring health care event; it also interfaces with almost all other aspects of our health care. For example, four out of five people who visit a physician leave with at least one prescription (*The Chain Pharmacy Industry Profile*, 2001). According to the World Health Organization, successful treatment depends more than all else on adherence to medication therapies

(World Health Organization, 2003). When we have a change in care, such as hospitalization, we become especially vulnerable to medical errors as a result of incomplete or inaccurate communication about our medication therapies. After hospital and intensive care unit discharges, we are at high risk of unintentionally discontinuing the medications that are proven to treat chronic diseases (Bell et al., 2011). Where a hospital readmission could have been avoided, there is a one in three chance that the readmission can be directly traced back to a medication-related event (van Walraven et al., 2011).

Almost all of us have used or will need to use a prescription drug at some time in our lives. The importance to us of medications is clear. However, when we use these powerful chemicals in our bodies, there is so much that can go wrong. Research has shown that having the right information, in the right amount, and at the right time is vital for using medications correctly; the information guides our decisions and changes our behaviors (Kemper & Metter, 2002). With good information, patients can often heal themselves. Without it, they can do themselves harm, overlook effective cures, and undermine the best-laid clinical plans (Kemper & Metter, 2002).

At the time this book is being written, there has been an information explosion in our society. A quick search on the Internet can find information about almost anything, including prescription drugs. Every time we purchase a medication, it comes with information on its label and attached to the container or bag in which it is sold. When Americans and Canadians settle down to watch television, advertisements for medications abound; many other developed countries have been debating whether to follow suit. Why not, you may ask. This is not 1964 and most of us today want to be informed about medicines. However, the way the information is provided and the language it uses can be confusing and sometimes quite overwhelming.

How did we get here? Why is the information given to us in this way? Where are we headed and what can we do about it? Those are questions we would like to address in this book.

THE AGE OF CHANGE AND PATIENT EMPOWERMENT?
THE PATIENT PACKAGE INSERT

The 1960s were a time of far-reaching change in the U.S. health care system. During this decade, Medicaid and Medicare were established as permanent fixtures. Ethical standards for health care providers changed from withholding information to giving information to patients. For example, up until 1965 the pharmacist code of ethics prohibited pharmacists from discussing the therapeutic purpose of the medications they were dispensing with patients. Today, it is considered a professional duty for pharmacists.

1968 was an annus mirabilis for patient empowerment, or so it promised to be. In that year, the Patient Package Insert was born. Patients being prescribed oral contraceptives and estrogens would henceforth, by Food and Drug Administration (FDA) regulation, receive an information leaflet to help them manage their medicine.

The 1970s came and went—but without the FDA mandating patient package inserts for a single other prescription drug. Finally, in September 1980, the FDA established rules and procedures for preparing and distributing patient package inserts for a limited number of prescription drugs. However, the FDA had neither the resources nor the motivation to develop these leaflets itself. This would be left to the pharmaceutical manufacturers, with the FDA just giving final approval (45 Federal Register, 1980).

Immediately, there was a chorus of protests. Pharmaceutical manufacturers, health care professional associations, and private-sector firms supplying patient information all insisted that, while they all favored patient package inserts, this would be done more effectively and creatively if only the FDA would not pass any regulations. In 1982, the regulations were revoked (47 Federal Register, 1982).

In the 1980s and early 1990s, the ball of prescription drug information was in the private sector's court. It began to generate a considerable range of patient package inserts and also worked on how best to present information on prescription containers and other "patient medication information" (PMI) resources. But the initial results were far from encouraging. The private sector could not figure out how to make this information practical or imaginative. In 1995, the FDA acted again. It was authorized to propose renewed regulations for written drug information that addressed both voluntary and mandatory aspects. First, it set two target dates to bring voluntary information leaflets up to an acceptable standard (60 Federal Register, 1995). The proposal was that, by 2000, 75% of people receiving new prescriptions would receive "useful written patient information" with them, and that by 2006 the target would increase to 95%. Second, the proposed rule also would require manufacturers to prepare and distribute approved "Medication Guides" for a limited number of prescription drugs that raised a significant public health concern.

But again, the same alliance of lobbyists geared up to hit back. Pharmacists and physicians warned that mandatory Medication Guides would impinge on clinical practice and clinical autonomy. Manufacturers fretted that giving out Medication Guides might persuade the courts that the physician was no longer a "learned intermediary" in the process and expose them to liability suits. At this point, for once, the U.S. Congress stepped in. In August 1996, while the FDA was still reviewing the public comments on the 1995 proposed rule, Congress enacted Public Law 104–180 (1996). This law endorsed the FDA's first objective: it set a target date to bring voluntary information leaflets up to an acceptable standard of usability and factuality. It also called for a committee of stakeholders to develop a long-range Action Plan, with the Secretary of Health and Human Services to provide oversight.

It was now almost three decades since the Patient Package Inserts had hit the pharmacies—and yet the pharmaceutical industry and the health care system were still at it with "action plans". The *Action Plan for the Provision of Useful Prescription Medicine Information* (1996) affirmed the FDA's goals for distribution of useful written patient information.

However, American health information advocates were to be disappointed once again. In 2000, the FDA commissioned a study to measure how well the private sector was meeting the interim goals of the Action Plan with a focus on distribution guidelines and quality of information content. The good news was that distribution guidelines (75% of all prescriptions by 2000) were exceeded, with 87% of prescriptions being accompanied by written consumer medication information (Svarstad, Bultman & Tabak, 2003). The bad news was that the quality of the information was poor and varied inexplicably from one pharmacy to the next. Although most information leaflets were judged to provide unbiased information, a majority of leaflets did not include adequate information about contraindications, precautions, and how to avoid harm. So more than 30 years had passed since the first patient package inserts, and no consumer-information standards had been implemented for drugs—the most potentially hazardous products regulated by the FDA (Shrank & Avorn, 2007).

And so the FDA was brought on again, at the behest of its Advisory Committee on Drug Safety and Risk Management. It moved to hold consultations and a public meeting—and then issued its first detailed guidance on the matter (Food and Drug Administration, 2006). This contained only non-binding recommendations related to such things as legibility, readability, precautions to include, and the reporting of clinical trial results.

The private sector had dropped the ball and the FDA attempted to pick it up. However, it was not allowed any part in refereeing this game. It was only a kind of honorary coach, and the players didn't much care for its wisdom when push came to shove. Recently published research shows that FDA guidance has largely been ignored, including matters of legibility, readability, quality of information, and reporting of clinical trials findings (Kimberlin & Winterstein, 2008; Schwartz & Woloshin, 2009; Winterstein, Linden, Lee, Fernandez & Kimberlin, 2010). A report on health literacy commissioned by the drug manufacturer Pfizer placed this all in a broader, but no less alarming context (Vernon, Trujillo, Rosenbaum, & DeBuono, 2007):

> At virtually every point along the healthcare services spectrum, the healthcare system behaves in a way that requires patients to read and understand important healthcare information. This information is dense, technical, and has jargon-filled language. Examples include completing health insurance applications, reading signs in hospitals and clinics about where to go and where to sign in, and following written and oral instructions in brochures and pamphlets, as well as prescription medication directions.

In June 2008, a broad-based group representing pharmacies, medical information companies, and consumer groups petitioned the FDA to design a "one-document solution" to replace the ragbag of patient package inserts, consumer medication information leaflets, and medication guides. The FDA acted in February 2009 when it moved forward with the goal of developing a model leaflet now dubbed "Patient Medication Information" (Food and Drug Administration, 2009a). Three prototype leaflets were commissioned, drawing upon empirical research on drug labeling. The prototypes were to be tested on real-life consumers (75 Federal Register, 2010). Revealingly, however, the most recent references the FDA could cite were from 12 years earlier, underscoring how slowly the field of patient medication information had advanced in the U.S.

The FDA proceeded with broad-based consultations and workshops, the emphasis being on tangible and pragmatic goals such as:

Creation of central and customized repositories for wording and content
Producing a popular lexicon of common terms
Improving legibility and comprehension
Collaboration among physicians, pharmacists, and information suppliers
Incentives for pharmacies to distribute patient medication information
Patient usability
Development of web-based as well as paper-based information.

The discussions revealed the gaps in the need for personalized information versus standardized information. While a short, standardized patient medication information leaflet would be more feasible, the FDA also acknowledged that no standardized reading matter will speak to all consumers of medication. Personalization is needed and the Web could be part of the solution.

At the time of writing, there is acknowledgment that the path taken regarding patient medication information since 1968 has done little to empower patients. Intelligent minds are still laboring at communicating drug benefits and risks and, even more fundamental, improving how patients make sense of written materials. To make wise decisions about using medications and to take them safely and appropriately, individuals must have an understanding of the risks, benefits, and directions for using them. To date, this information is inconsistent, incomplete, and difficult for the average American to read and understand (Shrank & Avorn, 2007; Vernon, Trujillo, Rosenbaum, & DeBuono, 2007).

Europe and Australia, by comparison, seemed to be doing the right things. Following British and German initiatives in the 1980–1990s (Glinert, 1998), the European Union legislated in 1999 that all medicines Europe-wide should have full and comprehensible patient leaflets, based on content and readability guidelines— and in 2005 took a leap forward by requiring that leaflets (usually manufacturer supplied) for all new drugs be user-tested (Raynor, 2013):

> The package leaflet shall reflect the results of consultations with target patient groups to ensure that it is legible, clear and easy to use.

Australia went down the same path in 2003 by requiring user-tested leaflets for all medicines—often printed out at the pharmacy (Raynor, 2003). The results, even prior to user-testing, seemed encouraging: An evaluation of usability and clinical content for four drugs gave the Australian leaflets a mean 90%, the British 81%, and the U.S. leaflets just 68% (Raynor et al., 2007).

However, there seems to be a gap between what experts say and users think. A Europe-wide survey (European Medicines Agency, 2009) revealed that the effective medication leaflet is still elusive. Most of the users surveyed did not think that leaflets were much help, with their complex language and layout. They still wanted to hear the information from their doctor or pharmacist. And if written information was to be of any use, it had to be tailored to their particular illness, it had to be both concise in parts and comprehensive in parts—and it also had to give guidance on whether to take medicine or not. Quite a tall order. There was more depressing news in a recent study of UK leaflets for antidepressants from pharmaceutical companies (Haw & Stubbs, 2011). Gaps and disparities abounded.

There is much about layout and language that cannot be encompassed in fixed templates or regulations for "plain English". Medical leaflets are more an art and a culture of communication than a procedure. These things take time and skill as well as political will.

Thus, the American health system's problems with written medication information must not be laid solely at the door of government and industry. There has been a failure all round on an international scale to interrogate the needs of end-users and to determine how best to meet them.

In what we have discussed so far, the main goal is consumer education. But there is another side to this coin: persuasion. Here, the manufacturers have not been coy. Indeed, they are leading the charge.

DIRECT-TO-CONSUMER ADVERTISING FOR PRESCRIPTION DRUGS

Practically every American adult has seen or heard an advertisement for a prescription drug. Each year, approximately one-third of adults in the United States talk to a prescriber about an advertised product. And a sizable minority actually asks for the medication and gets it - about five out of every 100 adults in the U.S (Schommer, Singh & Hansen, 2005). Not that they are sold on them: it appears that individuals who ask for and receive an advertised medication like to take a "toe-in-the-water" approach. That is, they want to try the medication to see if the product will work for them as advertised before jumping in all the way. Drug advertisers have had good reason to up the spending on such ads: Research shows that much of the time, patients report that the result was what they wanted (Glasgow, Schommer, Gupta & Pierson, 2002; Schommer, Singh & Hansen, 2005).

Industry has also been able to argue that it is good for the nation's health. According to one study, a sizable portion of patients who mentioned an advertised drug during a clinic visit saw their physician for clinically important conditions such as high cholesterol or high blood pressure, and many of these visits resulted in new diagnoses for significant health problems such as heart disease (Weissman et al., 2003). In addition, these so-called "direct-to-consumer advertising visits" often resulted in care that went beyond the expected prescribing of drugs, both advertised and not, such as follow-up tests and visits. When researchers studied the outcomes of these visits, they failed to find any significant negative health consequences among those patients who took an advertised drug. In fact, the researchers found a small advantage in the relief of side effects among patients who switched their medications to an advertised drug after their visit.

With encouraging results like this, it is easy to understand why pharmaceutical drug manufacturers would invest in direct-to-consumer advertising for their products. Early on, Alan Holmer wrote in the *Journal of the American Medical Association* (Holmer, 1999):

> Direct-to-consumer (DTC) advertising is an excellent way to meet the growing demand for medical information, empowering consumers by educating them about health conditions and possible treatments. By doing so, it can play an important role in improving health care.... DTC advertising that encourages millions of Americans to consult their physicians can help to improve public health because a number of leading diseases are under-diagnosed and under-treated.

With great news like this, why not let the marketplace take care of getting necessary drug information out to the public? Why all the fuss about Patient Medication Information leaflets when market-driven advertising could do the job?

As a channel for communicating the potential benefits of prescription drug products, advertising of prescription drugs directly to consumers (as against physicians) burgeoned. Direct-to-consumer advertising for prescription drug products was a mere $130 million in the United States during 1993, but by 2007 it had soared to $4.9 billion (Sepulveda Adams, 2013; Yuan, 2013) and it has been projected to reach $11.4 billion by 2017 (Global Industry Analysts, 2011).

If overall spending on direct-to-consumer advertising dropped between 2008 and 2012, it was because of the economic recession and the shortage of blockbuster prescription drugs in the marketplace (to which much of the advertising dollar is directed). Now, however, advertising has received a new boost. Internet advertising has emerged as a preferred communication medium and the fastest growing media channel for pharmaceuticals—although regulatory restrictions and uncertainties have been holding it back (Global Industry Analysts, 2011; PM360, 2013). For example, Internet advertising for prescription drugs in 2009 increased by 31% in just 12 months to $117.4 million, before falling back to $68.4 million in 2012, and projections are hard to make. In any event, the use of the Internet and social media websites as a source for health information has also grown exponentially (Lenhart, 2008), while Pharma marketers use every tactic that is legal to marry information and advertising. These emerging media have the advantages of targeting and orchestrating messages, establishing two-way dialogue, and personalizing advertisements for consumers.

However, the Internet has downsides of its own. Being able to target, orchestrate, personalize and establish two-way dialogue may be a benefit for health promotion, but how are we to protect consumers from false or misleading information that might be conveyed? And when it comes to information about prescription medications, to understand some of this information needs special training. And do the advertisements make full disclosure of benefits, risks, and costs? Without this, information can be presented in such a way as to mislead. Poor decisions will inevitably follow.

Here is an example of how a series of true statements could be misleading:

True Statement #1: According to the text book, *Harper's Biochemistry* (Murray, Granner, Mays & Rodwell, 1996), there are eight sugars that are essential to the human body.

True Statement #2: According to *Harper's Biochemistry*, only two or three of the necessary eight are commonly found in a Western diet.

True (but misleading statement): There is a product that can help provide you with the ability to get all eight of the sugars you need.

Erroneous Conclusion: You need to buy this product in order to get all eight of the sugars you need.

What was left unsaid is that the human body has the ability to synthesize all eight of the sugars, in the correct amounts (Schnarr & Freeze, 2008). Furthermore, the product for sale could have contained nothing more than simple table sugar and the misleading statement still would have been true.

DIRECT-TO-CONSUMER DRUG ADVERTISING ON THE TIGHTROPE

Direct-to-Consumer drug advertisers walk a tightrope. How can we maximize health promotion through the provision of useful information and minimize the need for consumer protection from false or misleading information?

By *health promotion* we have in mind the positive effects such advertising can have on some individuals' understanding of new or better treatments for their ailments, joint decision-making between physicians and patients, or quicker diffusion of new therapies for those who need them. *Consumer protection* is about minimizing any harm that drug advertising could inflict on vulnerable populations if the information conveyed in such advertising is not understood or if it would lead to detrimental decisions (e.g. inappropriate drug use, strained physician-patient relationships, etc.). This is where the U.S. Food and Drug Administration comes in—and with it, a pointer to where we are today and how we got here.

Under the Federal Food, Drug, and Cosmetic Act, the FDA is responsible for ensuring that the labeling and advertising of prescription drugs is truthful and not misleading. Section 502 (n) of the Act prohibits the advertising of drugs that is false or misleading or that fails to provide required information about product risks (66 Federal Register, 2001). Although prescription drug advertising was once for physicians' eyes only, the new vogue for health coverage in the Carter-Reagan era media and the FDA's matching new credo that people should be told about their pills, even (under strict controls) by marketers, begat the first mag ads and TV brand spots (Pines, 1999).

A draft and final *Guidance for Broadcast Advertising of Prescription Medicines* (Food and Drug Administration, 1997; 1999a) effectively opened the door for pharmaceutical companies to advertise prescription drug products directly to the United States public on television and radio. In the FDA guidance, three types of advertisements were identified. The first type of advertisement, called a "Reminder Ad", just lists the product name, not what it is used for. If a sponsor of an advertisement wants to place its product name on a pen, on a billboard, or any place else, it can do so without any further requirements for providing more information to the consumer.

The second type, called a "Help Seeking Ad," does not mention a product name, just that there is something to treat a specific condition. The advertisement could direct the consumer to talk to his or her physician to get more information. This advertisement is particularly useful when a new product comes to the market and is the only one of its kind for treating a condition. An example of this was a toenail fungus treatment that would treat the ailment by giving the medication internally and treating the fungus from the inside out rather than treating the ailment with externally applied remedies. Like the Reminder Ad, there were no further requirements for providing any more information to the consumer.

The final type of advertisement, called a "Product Claim Ad," includes both the name of the product *and* what it is used for. In this instance, the sponsor of the advertisement is required under FDA rule, as originally designed for print ads, to provide a "fair balance" of information between risks and benefits and to provide a so-called "brief summary." The "brief summary" is the technical name for detailed information that includes all the risks listed in the drug's prescribing information and at least one FDA-approved use of the drug. Generally, the "brief summary" includes information about (1) who should not take the drug, (2) when the drug should not be taken, (3) possible serious side effects of the drug, and (4) frequently occurring, but not necessarily serious, side effects. The "brief summary" is quite long and is written using medical terminology. For direct-to-consumer advertising, the FDA encourages the sponsors of the ads to use language consumers can understand, but this is not a requirement. If you look at a print ad for a drug product, the 'brief summary' is usually written in black and white, using small type, and takes up a whole page.

However, giving a "brief summary" in broadcast advertisements was never feasible, since these last only 30 to 60 seconds. So in 1997, the FDA allowed a new way for providing this information. Broadcast advertisements could now present a "fair balance" of risks and benefits by just making a "major statement" about the most important risks associated with using the product. They also had to make "adequate provision" for disseminating the brief summary labeling—through concurrently running print ads, a toll free phone number, a website, and a statement about talking with your physician or pharmacist.

Belatedly, in May 2009, the FDA also added that such ads should use "language that is readily understandable by consumers" and "avoid the use of vague terms or explanations that are readily subject to different interpretations."

In Chapter 6 we will take a closer and more critical look at TV drug commercials and the way in which marketers have been able to tilt the "balance" between promotion and information.

How does the Internet fit into all this? In November 2009, the FDA held public hearings on the promotion of drugs on the Internet and other new media tools. At the time this chapter is being written, the same rules that applied to broadcast advertising are being applied to Internet and social media channels. However, an interesting interpretation for Internet advertising is the so-called "one click rule": hyperlinks cannot be used to "click away" from a web page that gives the benefits information of a drug product to find information about the risks. To do so would not meet FDA requirements for fair balance of both risks and benefits to be listed on the same web page.

It is noteworthy that there is no pre-screening or pre-approval of direct-to-consumer advertisements for prescription drugs. The FDA only sends Notices of Violation to drug manufacturers if there is a problem *after* the advertisements have been printed, posted, or aired.

Clearly, the FDA has invested far more time and money in drug advertising than in drug information. But where we are today with drug advertising in the media is a result of a series of "patches": (a) The FDA rules in force for prescription drug advertising were written with health professionals, not the public, in mind; (b) these rules were first designed for printed ads and modified bit by bit over time for use with broadcast media. Furthermore, (c) the FDA decided that there were really three different types of ad, and only the "Product Claim" ad needed to provide the viewer with balanced risk information.

In its defense, however, the FDA over the years has used a cautious, carefully thought out, "slowly-slowly" approach when it comes to oversight of advertising for prescription drugs (Chelimsky, 1991a, 1991b; Food and Drug Administration, 1999b, 2000; Aikin, 2002). There has been a balance between health promotion through the dissemination of useful information and the need for consumer protection from false or misleading claims (Kaphingst & DeJong, 2004). Care has been taken to protect commercial freedoms of speech (Carver, 2008), and thought has been devoted to ways of applying these rules to the new media as they develop.

There has been no consideration, however, of how all of this affects health care costs. The FDA is not allowed to focus on that.

THE OUTCOMES OF DRUG ADVERTISING: HOW MUCH DO WE KNOW?

It has been half a generation since the 1997 ruling that allowed prescription drug advertising over American radio and TV, and later through the Internet and social media. What have been the controversies? What evidence is there for how this approach has been working?

$1.9 billion was spent on direct-to-consumer advertising in 1999, generating an estimated $9 billion in product sales. From that early experience in broadcast advertising of prescription medications, billions of dollars have been devoted to this channel of communication in order to create awareness for newly approved drug products and to create brand loyalty for drug products that have their patents due to expire. In either case, the advertised products tend to be among the most expensive in their therapeutic category. Scrutiny and criticism have come from many directions (Auton, 2004; Main, Argo, & Huhmann, 2004; Wilkes, Bell & Kravitz, 2000). Some are concerned that the growth of direct-to-consumer advertising is encouraging the use of relatively expensive prescription drugs when less expensive alternatives would work. Meanwhile, the overall goal of FDA policy regarding such advertising is to protect and promote public health by the dissemination of truthful, balanced, and accurately communicated information about prescription drug products.

FDA has no mandate or authority to establish rules regarding the costs of medications. Thus, this objection is not addressed in FDA rules.

Others have proposed that while advertising may alert consumers to new information and facilitate treatment of their medical problems, it also may confuse many consumers and adversely impact the relationship between patients and their health care providers. How then can such advertising maximize informational benefits while minimizing potentially misleading or confusing messages?

Another consideration is whether advertising trivializes medication use to the point where individuals view medications as having no risks. Consumers may falsely believe that drug advertisements are pre-screened by the government and that only the "completely safe" and "most effective" drugs may be advertised. Individuals who request medications based on advertising tend to have favorable views of such advertising. They are, of course, also optimistic about influencing their physician. Could the messages they get from ads be contributing to their views?

Is the "toe-in-the-water" approach to prescription drug use appropriate? The idea of trying different medications until the best one is found before jumping in all the way could be wasteful and dangerous. Surely it's better to go with evidence-based comparative effectiveness and the clinical judgment of a physician. However, the idea of working with patients to find therapies that fit their needs, wants, and lifestyles does have merit.

Another concern relates to the notion of "medicalizing normal human experience." That is, misleading consumers to believe that there is a "pill for every ill", or even worse, to lead them to believe that they suffer from an "ill for every pill" that they see advertised. Furthermore, advertising could contribute to the "minimization of healthy living" in which consumers no longer strive to practice healthy lifestyles because they think that there are medications that can overcome the consequences of unhealthy lifestyles.

Looming over all of this is the content of these ads. The Council on Ethical and Judicial Affairs of the American Medical Association adopted this unambiguous resolution (2000):

> Many broadcast advertisements are misleading, using imagery to suggest effectiveness far beyond what clinical evidence suggests.

The FDA has recognized the problem—at times. Regulators have sent formal warning letters to sponsors of some direct-to-consumer advertisements that were judged as having confusing or misleading information for consumers. One example relates to the use of imagery in an inappropriate manner in which the audio presentation of the major risk information associated with the use of a drug product included visual presentations of falling matches, a falling lighter, and falling cigarettes. The appearance of these visual presentations was judged to interfere with the viewers' ability to listen to and process the information in the audio presentation that disclosed the most important risks associated with the drug product. Thus, the risk information was not presented with a prominence reasonably comparable to the presentation of the effectiveness of the drug.

Warning letters sent by the FDA typically have related to: (1) unsubstantiated or misleading claims, (2) inadequate or minimized risk information, (3) absence of a "brief summary" giving full details (in print ads), (4) absence of "adequate provision" of a source for full details (in broadcast ads), (5) inadequate or no fair balance, (6) non-disclosure of a health care professional as an additional source of information, and (7) obscurity.

In light of these problems, some have called for more changes in FDA rules. Their recipe would include:

1. balance the risk and benefit information more effectively in TV ads
2. always use consumer-friendly language
3. give sources of additional information in both audio and visual channels
4. provide more information about the portrayed indication
5. evaluate consumers' comprehension of direct-to-consumer advertising, and
6. require prior approval of advertisements.

It has been suggested that the FDA could use technology to identify advertisements that are likely to be harmful to the public, use quality control processes in their reviews, and make judgments based more on scientific information about how people receive, process, and use information for making decisions (Morris & Pines, 2000).

At this point, after years of advertising and testing, how much do we know? A major review (2010) was published by Frosch, Grande, Tarn & Kravitz of the empirical evidence for and against prescription drug advertising. Their results were mixed. They categorized the evidence into five areas: (1) educational value, (2) contributions to the quality of clinical care, (3) effects on patient adherence, (4) promotion of questionable prescribing practices, and (5) over-diagnosis and medicalization. Here is what they found:

1. Educational Value

Consumer surveys have shown that prescription drug advertising provides information that is valued by the public, but there is insufficient evidence to conclude that ads are an effective educational vehicle. Ads tend to overemphasize benefits and minimize or obscure risks. Consumers with average health literacy capabilities may find information in ads hard to understand and could be misled. Further, the way ads are designed may intentionally maximize recall of benefit information and minimize recall of risk information.

2. Contributions to the Quality of Clinical Care

There is evidence that prescription drug advertising can improve the quality of clinical care. Studies showed that ads encourage discussion of therapeutic options between physicians and patients. Also, ads may increase the treatment of some health care conditions that typically go undertreated. However, for some patients and physicians, prescription drug advertising can strain the physician-patient relationship and could adversely affect the quality of patient care.

3. Effects on Patient Adherence

When patients do not take their medications as prescribed, the potential benefits of the therapy are not achieved. This is referred to as "non-adherence with therapy" and costs approximately $100 billion annually in lost productivity and added health care expenditures such as hospitalization. Some have proposed that prescription drug advertising can increase a person's positive views and loyalty to a drug product and thus, improve adherence. The evidence to date is scant and suggests that advertising may have small, beneficial effects on drug adherence for advertised products.

4. Promotion of Questionable Prescribing Practices

A chief concern is the potential for prescription drug advertising to increase inappropriate prescribing. There are both cost and safety concerns. Advertised products typically are for brand name products (patent-protected products for which there is no generic version available). Prescription drug advertising is most often used for a product launch in which the goal is to build awareness and recognition of the product as it is introduced to the market. Also, advertising is used for products just before their patent is due to expire so that brand loyalty can be built, with the aim of keeping market share as generic competition enters the marketplace.

These patent-protected brand name products are relatively expensive vis-à-vis comparable drugs. In some cases, the advertised products are riskier to use as well. Critics argue that when one considers effectiveness, safety, and cost, oftentimes there are better alternatives to the advertised product (Kjos, Schommer & Yuan, 2010).

After careful review of the evidence, Frosch and his colleagues concluded that prescription requests prompted by advertising increase both appropriate and inappropriate prescribing. You might benefit—or you might be worse off. Which is the more probable remains unclear.

5. Over-Diagnosis and Medicalization

Critics of prescription drug advertising are concerned that it leads to "medicalization", the process by which nonmedical problems come to be defined as treatable illnesses. They argue that the widening of what constitutes illness is more about expanding markets and sales of products than improving population health. Some propose that there are natural consequences of the human condition (experiencing short-term grief, mood swings, changes in sexual drive) and the aging process (wrinkles, hair loss, changes in hormone levels, changes in muscle tone) that should be embraced as part of the life journey rather than being identified as a disease that warrants pharmaceutical treatment.

And indeed, Frosch and colleagues found that prescription drug advertising does medicalize symptoms previously not defined as illness. However, whether a net social benefit exists is a complex cultural and political question. Studies that simply describe the presence of such a phenomenon do not offer a straightforward answer in this case.

WHY IS THERE SUCH A MIXED REVIEW?

The evidence just reviewed shows that one can find both positive and negative outcomes from direct-to-consumer advertising. Whether the positives outweigh the negatives, no one knows for sure. We are right back to the dilemma of trying to maximize health promotion versus minimizing the need for consumer protection. Why is there such a mixed review on prescription drug advertising?

In our judgment, a one-size-fits-all approach will affect individuals differently depending on who you are. The evidence just described provides an overview of the effects that prescription drug advertising has had on the U.S. adult population. However, it is important to note that although most Americans have seen this type of advertising, they do not respond to it uniformly.

In a study published in the *International Journal of Advertising*, Hugh White and colleagues expanded our understanding about what actions might be taken by individuals in response to ads (White, Draves, Soong & Moore, 2004). Actions reported by respondents during the previous 12 months as a result of seeing or hearing ads were quite diverse and included:

> made an appointment with a doctor (39%)
> purchased a non-prescription drug product (36%)
> resumed taking a prescription drug they already had (36%)
> called for prescription refill (33%)
> used a coupon for an advertised prescription drug (20%)
> asked a doctor to prescribe a specific prescription drug (13%).

People are different and they have different needs, wants, and situations.

White and colleagues acknowledged that "not everyone responds to drug information in the same way". To help understand different segments of the American population in terms of how they may respond to ads, they conducted a statistical analysis of consumer characteristics and identified four broad groups, based on how they respond to health information and advertising of health-related products.

51% are "the Healthy Half". They have no obvious health problems and little interest in health information from any source.

28% are the "Doctor Led", who often discuss advertised medicines with their doctors, but defer to their advice.

13% are "Self-Managers". They have the occasional ailment, which they tend to self-treat with over-the-counter meds.

8% are "Solution Seekers," with health problems which they proactively research.

There are further differences even among the people most likely to respond to advertising. Some are only *searchers* (those who ask questions and gather information), and some are *requesters* (those who actually ask for a prescription). Some individuals search out information about advertised drugs simply as a way to stay informed about their health. The most distinguishing characteristics of these individuals are that they take a relatively large number of medications daily and pay a relatively large amount out of pocket for their medications (Schommer,

Singh & Hansen, 2005). This group might consist of members of the Doctor-Led cluster mentioned earlier. They want to stay informed, but they leave the decision about which medication is prescribed to their physician.

The individuals who actually request medications based on advertising tend to have several distinguishing characteristics. They are more likely to view advertising as beneficial, they have a good relationship with and can influence their physician, and they consider medications valuable and relatively easy to use. These traits are quite consistent with the description of the Solution Seeker segment of the population. The 8% of adults who make up this segment of the population could very well be the patients who ask for advertised medications during physician visits.

It is possible that advertising may influence only a small segment of the patient population in the United States. Given this, one might be tempted to conclude that advertising poses minimal risk to public health. After all, it appears to affect a relatively small percentage of the population who happen to value such advertising and say they benefit from the information it contains.

However, a number of unanswered questions remain. For example, will the distribution of the Healthy Half, Doctor-Led, Self-Managers, and Solution Seekers change over time? With the aging of the baby boomers, Gen Xers, and Millennials, will the percentage of the population who are Solution Seekers increase in future years? If yes, then what effect will drug advertising have on public health? Will a greater proportion of the U.S. population expect a "pill for every ill" or, worse, think that they have an "ill that fits every pill" that they see advertised?

Advertising of prescription drugs is considered a useful and appreciated information source for a segment of the population. Even if it were banned in the United States (as it currently is in every other country except New Zealand), people who make up the Solution Seeker cluster still would likely obtain information about newly approved medications through other sources, such as the Internet, word of mouth, and articles in the popular press.

WHAT ABOUT NEW ZEALAND?

As just mentioned, New Zealand is the only country other than the United States that does not ban direct-to-consumer advertising for prescription drugs. When New Zealand enacted statutes regarding the distribution of promotional material for prescription drugs in its 1981 Medicines Act and its 1984 Medicines Regulation, it did not consider the possibility of consumer-directed promotions. It focused on technical information that would be distributed to health care providers and payers for health care. Furthermore, the New Zealand Bill of

Rights Act 1990 explicitly protected freedom of speech, including commercial free speech. Pharmaceutical companies viewed this statute as being similar to the First Amendment of the U.S. Constitution which also has been interpreted as protecting commercial free speech.

With this legal environment in place, direct-to-consumer advertising for prescription drugs began in New Zealand in the early 1990s, and by the end of the decade it became widespread. Growing concern triggered a New Zealand Ministry of Health public consultation that was held in March 2006. Shortly thereafter, the New Zealand Ministry of Health (2006) published its report. This comprehensive review addressed seven aspects of drug advertising, identifying negatives and positives similar to those voiced in the United States.

1. Provision of Health Care Information to Consumers

Negatives

- Advertising is about increasing sales; misrepresents the benefits of a product and downplays the risks; is inappropriate for prescription medicines; fails to present independent sources of information.

Positives

- The public have a desire and a right to information.
- Advertising can improve knowledge of available treatments, and prompt discussion and adherence.
- It is the role of the prescriber to provide full information and prescribe appropriately.

2. The Appropriate and Quality Use of Medicines

Negatives

- Advertising can lead to pressure being put on prescribers and promotes the use of new medicines over older medicines with established safety profiles.
- There is no evidence of health benefit from advertising, but there are concerns about its negative health impact.

Positives

- Advertising may result in earlier diagnosis and treatment.
- Inappropriate prescribing, if it occurs, is due to poor prescriber "gate-keeping."

3. Practicable and Cost-Effective Regulation

Negatives

- The current system is ineffective and not transparent, and does not reflect the risks of prescription medicines.
- Advertising on the Internet cannot be regulated.
- Self-regulation does not address the purported negative effects of advertising—the only solution is a complete ban.

Positives

- The current system of self-regulation is adequate and flexible, and ensures a high level of responsibility and compliance; more regulation would discourage Industry.
- Consumers have a right to access pharmaceutical information via advertising.

4. Appropriate and Proper Standards for Prescription Medicine Advertising

Negatives

- It is not possible to meet the information needs of consumers via advertising.
- Even if standards are set according to public health interests, Industry will continue to "push the envelope".

Positives

- Current advertising standards are appropriate and ensure a high level of responsibility and compliance.
- Advertising should not be considered any differently from any other form of advertising.
- Advertising is only one part of a marketing mix—if regulations are increased, companies will find other ways to disseminate information about their products.

5. Medicalization

Negatives

- Advertising encourages people to perceive normal bodily and ageing processes as illnesses.
- Advertising promotes pharmaceutical treatments over other alternatives that may be better and less open to medical misadventure.

Positives

- Lifestyle and ageing treatments now attract different cultural attitudes, and can improve quality of life and health.
- Advertising identifies under-diagnosed and under-treated conditions.
- Appropriate prescribing by general practitioners reduces the potential for medicalization.

6. Impact on Patient-Doctor Relationships

Negatives

- Advertising fuels patients' expectations of making their own decisions, pressurizes physicians to prescribe a particular product, wastes consultation time, and can threaten the doctor-patient relationship.

Positives

- Advertising can assist doctor-patient dialogue, as patients do not usually exert pressure for a particular product and doctors are trained to prescribe a product only when appropriate.
- The dynamic between patients and doctors is changing, with consumers becoming more empowered and active in decisions concerning their health care.

7. Fiscal Pressures and Costs to Consumers

Negatives

- Advertising leads to unnecessary expenditure on medicines and consults, and can trigger resource allocation distortions.
- There is a clear relationship between advertising and increased pharmaceutical expenditure.

Positives

- Government has strict control of the pharmaceutical budget.
- Public health should transcend the financial position of the funder.

Four options emerged for further discussion:

1. Allow advertising to continue with more stringent regulation.
2. Allow advertising but with stricter requirements than specified by the Therapeutic Products Advertising Code.

3. Ban advertising and regulate disease-state advertising.
4. Ban advertising and ban for-profit disease-state advertising.

At the time of the writing of this chapter, no conclusive action has been taken in New Zealand.

WHAT ABOUT THE REST OF THE WORLD?

In other countries, where prescription drug advertising is prohibited, messages containing health-related information are still distributed. In these markets, however, advertisers promote disease management, health education, and other resources for patients. They also invite targeted groups of patients to visit websites that will provide information about clinics and practitioners who will provide the advertised services or pharmaceuticals. Using this approach, the marketers of prescription drugs can orchestrate campaigns in which the clinics and practitioners will be ready to prescribe their products when contacted by patients. There is some evidence to suggest that this orchestrated approach results in a greater return on investment than mass-market drug advertising in the United States.

While most countries are maintaining the status quo on their bans of direct-to-consumer advertising for prescription drugs, a flurry of activity has been undertaken recently in Europe. In light of consumers' desire for information about prescription medicines, the distribution of health-related information already taking place, and the right to commercial free speech, a proposal to change the rules on providing medicine information to patients was included in the "pharmaceutical package" presented by the European Commission (Commission of the European Communities, 2008). These measures would have allowed pharmaceutical companies to provide information on prescription medicines directly to consumers for the first time in Europe via the Internet and health publications, but not via TV or radio. Critics argued that the law requiring factual information did not guarantee "reliable and comparative information" and failed to protect the wider public from being targeted with prescription-only medicines advertising disguised as "information" (Medicines in Europe Forum, 2012).

Proponents pointed out that quality information in all European Union languages should be provided so that consumers are not taken in by poor-quality online information.

In September 2010 the European Parliament proposed tightening the European Commission proposals, by having regulatory agencies pre-screen the information produced by drug companies before it is made available to the public. Then, in October 2011, in the face of ongoing opposition from European member states, the Commission backed down on allowing drug company information to appear in the printed media. At the time of writing this chapter, the proposals have not even been examined by member states, thus delaying any further action. Meanwhile, the European Court of Justice ruled (C-316/09, 5 May 2011) that uploading a package leaflet at a passive link is not in violation but rewriting it for advertising purposes decidedly is.

So advertising is still considered an inappropriate means for pharmaceutical companies to communicate with patients in Europe because such communication bypasses the healthcare professional. Currently in Europe, as we mentioned earlier in this chapter, pharmaceutical manufacturers produce patient leaflets as an insert inside all medicine packs. These leaflets are created using a template and must involve consultation with target patient groups to ensure that the information is legible, clear and easy to use, before a license will be granted. This information, however, is only provided in combination with the dispensing of the product (Raynor, 2013).

Thus, the most important issue may not be whether prescription drug advertising is good or bad or whether it should be allowed or restricted. Rather, we should be planning and preparing for the waves of highly informed, assertive, and involved patients that we will encounter more and more often in the future.

MIGRATING TO THE WEB

Part of this planning must consider the recent explosion in the use of the Internet and social media—and their strong and often unanticipated effect on information and promotion.

According to Prevention Magazine's 13th annual national survey (Rodale, 2010), only 37% of the responders had "seen or heard" online risk information compared with 54% who had "seen or heard" online benefit information regarding prescription drugs—despite the FDA's requirement of "fair balance" between risk and benefit information. This compares poorly with the attention consumers have been and still are paying to both benefit and risk information in traditional media—print and broadcast ads. The difference is due to the familiarity of the traditional media and the recognizable formula, namely the use of the black and white page for print ads and the voice-over in broadcast ads.

The social media have catapulted in importance. Sixty percent of online consumers use social media when searching for health information. The Internet's rapidly multiplying user-generated content websites are being viewed as a trusted source of information by consumers, with Wikipedia and online forums or message boards achieving particular popularity. In the same Prevention Magazine survey, 76% of online users wanted to obtain information via the social media from other people who shared the same medical condition, 73% from doctors or other health care providers, and 66% from friends and family.

What are these consumers looking for?

- 78% seek information about a specific medical condition.
- 63% look at information about alternative treatments.
- 24% look for rankings, reviews and /or prescription medicine.

Overall, 62% of online consumers reported that the health information is useful and 58% say that the information is trustworthy. At the same time, 62% of online consumers are not interested in hearing from pharmaceutical companies.

Pharmaceutical manufacturers are working diligently to take advantage of online communication tools—they are desperate to improve the negative image that consumers have of them. As we mentioned, in 2009 Internet advertising for prescription drugs saw strong growth over 2008 (31% increase to $117.4 million). When one conducts a Google search in the U.S.A. for any of the top prescription drug products using the brand name, the manufacturer sponsored website (<brandname>.com) almost always is the second site listed. When one visits a manufacturer-sponsored website, the web designs are aesthetically pleasing and filled with a great deal of information.

But it also appears that pharmaceutical manufacturers realize that a great deal of work is yet to be done in order to meet the ever-changing FDA guidelines— and to become a preferred source of information. One need only eavesdrop on a pharmaceutical newsletter (PharmaLive), designed for pharmaceutical executives, to get the point:

> The entire direct-to-consumer business is in flux because consumers are changing the way they research and find information. Healthcare consumers are no longer simply passive receivers of print or television advertising. Most healthcare consumers are active researchers. [...]

> Because consumers have become more participatory in their health by asking questions and discussing symptoms, treatment options, and drug effectiveness in online forums, ... brands have an opportunity to perfect their listening skills ... Brands need to realize that they are guests at the party. ... They can be participants and contributors to the conversation, but they can't control it. For marketers used to controlling the brand messaging, this can be a difficult transition. (PharmaLive, 2010a)

Ultimately, though, the Industry is upbeat about the online era:

> One of the paradoxes of social media and alternative media channels is that on the one hand, studies show that patients trust what their peers say over claims made by

Pharma, yet on the other hand, consumer health sites can be filled with inaccurate or misleading information ... This is where Pharma could provide value... There are opportunities for brands to co-develop social media consumer programs with patient advocacy associations that provide reliable health information, build trust with patients, and help gain access to prescribers. (PharmaLive, 2010b)

All the evidence shows that pharmaceutical companies are devoting a great deal of thought and effort to developing new direct-to-consumer promotion strategies for their products. With the FDA still applying old rules to new challenges, while consumers flock to websites for health care and prescription drug information, and pharmaceutical companies try to balance compliance with FDA guidelines with the need for competitive advantage in the marketplace for their products, the next era of direct-to-consumer promotion for prescription drugs will be dynamic and full of potential peril.

Little research is devoted to web-based advertising for prescription drugs. Some of our initial work in this realm (Glinert & Schommer, 2010; Glinert 2010) reviewed and analyzed the 'official' company websites for the 100 top-selling drugs of 2009. We found that:

- there was little consistency or logical organization in the design of these websites that might have given a sense of coherence or frame of reference for handling the website.
- information and promotion mixed unpredictably, which could lead to confusion.
- any voice of authority or token of credibility was kept well in the background and often quite vague. There was little reference to expert opinion.
- benefit information was more prominent than risk information—prejudicing the FDA's requirement of fair balance.

Not only is there continued controversy regarding the effects of direct-to-consumer advertising of prescription drugs through print and broadcast media, but there will be new, more significant challenges for advertising that makes use of websites.

WHO ARE THE KEY PLAYERS?

So far, we have described the paths taken for *Patient Medication Information* and *Direct-to-Consumer Advertising* for prescription drugs. These paths have been directed by the balance between agencies' health promotion and consumer protection mandates. Both pathways have been fragmented and incremental in nature. Consumers have been walking through a dense jungle without clear direction, having to clear away vines and brush each step of the way.

However, these pathways have now in fact met, with Web-based sites becoming the point of convergence. Information and promotion are now coming together at this one place, in such a way as to make educational versus promotional sites difficult to distinguish. For each pathway, agencies such as the FDA have preferred to sidestep the Internet issue. As we will show in later chapters, prescription drug websites are already blurring the distinction between educational and promotional messages. Emerging from a dense jungle, we have reached a deep divide. There are several key players who will determine how we get across—or whether we do.

The Food and Drug Administration (and Similar Agencies in Other Countries)

The FDA is chronically bureaucratic, inefficient, and underfunded. In addition to its lack of foresight regarding prescription drug information and promotion, it suffers from dysfunction in other areas for which it has responsibility. These include: lengthy drug approval backlogs, delinquent manufacturing facility inspections, and lack of punishment for egregious marketing compliance misconduct (Wokasch, 2010). However, we would like to emphasize that extremely talented and energetic individuals work at the FDA. The challenge for the Agency is meeting the overwhelming expectations placed upon it within its limited budget and almost non-existent authority in many sectors of the marketplace.

Pharmaceutical Manufacturers

Pharmaceutical manufacturers are often described as greedy corporations that operate under a culture of "institutionalized deception" (Elliott, 2010), with an arsenal of questionable tactics such as:

1. withholding full disclosure of information for clinical trials
2. using ghost writers to write "scientific articles" with key opinion leaders' names attached to them
3. employing public relations specialists to manufacture "news" bulletins
4. incentivizing sales representatives to do practically anything to meet sales quotas
5. hiring "thought leaders" as consultants to travel the world to enlighten the medical community about the wonders of their new product
6. paying "hidden rebates" to health insurance companies in return for preferred placement on formularies

7. paying subsidiaries of insurance companies for research in exchange for preferred placement on formularies
8. paying generic manufacturers to withhold a generic going to market that would replace a brand product.

Again, we would be the first to acknowledge that extremely talented and energetic individuals are at work at these companies. The challenge for pharmaceutical manufacturers is meeting the overwhelming expectations placed upon them by shareholders in this high-risk, high-reward enterprise—while also working under the paralyzing regulations placed upon this industry. Unfortunately, new drug pipelines have recently dwindled. Few truly innovative products are being introduced into clinical practice. Revenue growth in the pharmaceutical industry has slowed, public trust has diminished, and there is a transitioning to an era of lowered expectations for this industry (Wokasch, 2010).

Health Care Insurers and Providers

Health insurance and provider organizations are under extreme pressure to generate profits. Health care reform has resulted in new payment and delivery models for health care, called Accountable Care Organizations (ACOs). This is a reimbursement model that links provider reimbursements to quality and performance metrics and also to reductions in the total cost of care for an assigned population of patients. Fee-for-service contracts are giving way to pay-for-performance contracts. As this model of payment emerges, the use of prescription drugs will be based on evidence about how effective a particular medication is, compared to alternatives. Large organizations will be crafting contracts based on "bang for their buck".

This raises some uncomfortable questions: What are the real motives behind the provision of prescription drug information? Will information be developed that persuades you to use a drug product that was deemed superior by a "comparative-effectiveness" study? Some executives are quite honest about it. They don't care about how well a prescription drug will work for a patient—they only care about what it will cost their company or what it will mean to their overall reimbursement. So here is another competing incentive to deal with. As we raise this issue, we would echo what we said about the Pharma industry: Passionate and reflective individuals work at health care insurer and provider companies. The challenge for them is in fulfilling the expectations of shareholders—and meeting shadowy pay-for-performance goals to maximize reimbursement.

Patients

Let us not forget the patients. Our own research has taught us that patients vary widely in their make-up, their preferences, and their needs. Some patients don't want to receive any information from others about their meds while others desire to take an active role in making decisions about them. Some people want information about effects of medications and others want to know about safety. In addition, when people seek information about medicines, there is a high likelihood that they will involve a personal contact, either lay or professional, in their search. This all underlines the importance of social networks in the decisions we make about prescription drugs.

Thus, 'one-size-fits-all' is probably not the best approach for disseminating patient medication information or promoting the product. Better, instead, to use what marketers call 'consumer segmentation', geared to desired levels of consumer involvement in the decision process. We should also acknowledge that we have different abilities, motivations, and needs when it comes to information. The challenge, then, is to meet the needs of each individual. And let's be honest: Most of us would rather think about something other than medications. When it comes to paying attention to our health care appointments and our medications, we get lazy and try to avoid those kinds of things. After all, we have more important things to do. How does one design and distribute medication information to a population that would prefer to watch television or read a book than spend time learning about prescription drugs?

CHAPTER TWO

Welcome to a Prescription Drug Site

WHO USES PRESCRIPTION DRUG SITES, HOW AND WHY?

A single decade has seen sweeping changes in the way consumers use the Internet and what they read there about their health.

The numbers of people with 24/7 broadband connection has soared. Audio and video content is as common as the written word. Many now spend more time with their iPads and smart phones on the Mobile Web than they do on the 'traditional' Web. The ways of adding your own individual voice to the Web have multiplied, and countless people are sharing theirs, via blogs, forums, YouTube, Facebook, tweets and the rest—the so-called social media. The power of search engines and wikis sits astride all this information, seemingly fashioning it into instant intelligence.

Reading health advice plays a valued part in life online. The Pew American Life survey of Internet use in 2013 (Fox & Duggan, 2013) reported that 59% of American adults had looked online for health information in the past year. Thirty-five percent said they had gone online specifically to try to figure out what medical condition they or someone else might have. And the experience was apparently quite a positive one. According to an American Life survey of 2011, 30% of American adults said that they, or someone they knew, had been helped by following health information on the Web. Just 3% of adults said that such health information had caused any harm (Fox, 2011). Similarly, a German survey in 2004 already found that three out of four German Internet-users had used it for health information (Dutta-Bergman, 2004)—although it was not the Germans' #1 source of health information (Dumitru et al., 2007).

The World Wide Web was a timely gift for the Health Consumer generation. Never before has the developed world had such instant and seemingly easy access to so much guidance about health in general and prescription drugs in particular. And what was yesterday's New World—a patient surfing the Internet at a home computer at 14 megabits per second—is now being eclipsed by the sight of patients in their doctor's waiting room using their smartphones and iPads to scan a bar code, open a Web page, or send a text message about a treatment option to a Pharma company's experts.

Similarly, never before have consumers *wanted* so much information about their medications. Two generations ago, drug information lay hidden away in the Physicians' Desk Reference, and there was no public clamor to reveal it. Today, however, consumer information is a right and an expectation, and the health system has followed suit. Public discourse mirrors this: We are all represented as health 'consumers', 'partnering' with our 'health care providers' (as doctors, pharmacists and nurses are known).

Where are we going for the facts about our medications? Surveys confirm that substantial numbers are finding the facts online. Thirty percent of users of About. com, America's third most visited general reference site, have reported researching the medication online before filling the prescription (About.com, 2010). We can translate that number into a percentage of Americans: 18% of American adults have consulted online reviews of particular drugs or medical treatments, according to the 2011 survey by the Pew Internet and American Life Project—and for caregivers the figure is over 25% (Fox, 2011).

However, it would be foolish to assume that this number is only headed upwards. A remarkable 25% decline was registered between 2010 and 2011 in the number of Americans searching the Internet for prescription drug information (Rodale, 2011). In the course of this book, we offer evidence as to the quality of drug information that the public is finding there.

Meanwhile, there appears to be widespread popular complacency about the reliability of medications. A national sample found that 39% of Americans mistakenly believe that the FDA approves only "extremely effective" drugs. Perhaps even more disturbing, one in four Americans mistakenly believes that the FDA approves only drugs without serious side effects (Schwartz & Woloshin, 2011). This kind of consumer is in urgent need of education.

A central element in any such evaluation is what people are looking for when they interrogate the Web about prescription drugs—and who they are doing this for.

The drug information seeker is in all likelihood a patient, a caregiver or a potential patient. They may have specific interests: They may be worried about having or contracting an ailment—and links about specific ailments will often bring them to information about specific drugs or even to a brand drug site. They may have been prescribed a drug and want more information about its effectiveness or side effects, how to take it, and what precautions to take. Or their interest may altogether be a more casual one. They may be at work or at home, in the pharmacy line or the doctor's waiting room.

A review of the research in America, Australia and the UK has confirmed some common sense expectations (Raynor et al., 2007):

People value drug information that reflects their particular ailment
They want a balance of information about the benefits and the risks
They vary in their need and desire for detail
They want information both to help decide about starting the drug and to advise them once they are taking it

Some insight into why people visit brand drug sites was provided by Manhattan Research (2011) in January 2011. The most common reasons given were:

Takes the product	33%
Just wants information	30%

The next most common reasons given were:

Just wants side-effect information	17%
Formerly took the product	15%
Takes another product for this condition	13%
Has the condition but doesn't take a prescription drug for it	12%

Sixty-six percent declared that they were looking just for themselves. Of those looking for someone else, half were looking on behalf of immediate family.

However, the Health Web isn't just about information or promotion. A rapidly growing number of consumers are going online to *manage* their health. To quote again from Manhattan Research (as cited by Malloy, 2011):

Some pharma companies are taking cues from Zappos and Best Buy's Twelpforce [...] For instance, Astra Zeneca's *My Measures for Success* program allows asthma and COPD sufferers to customize their own suite of tools and services to help them cope with the everyday issues of their condition, such as pollen counts and remembering to take their medication.

As a result, Pharma companies are increasingly talking about wrapping their brand message in a thick veil of "engagement"—mixing promotion with health services, information, and just about anything that will "engage" their target audience.

Critical to understanding how people use the Health Web is the distinction between "expert" and "lay", or common-sense, matters. For the latter, the American public is not limiting itself to websites maintained by health professionals. The Pew Internet and American Life Project survey reported (Fox, 2011):

> When the item involved technical issues related to a health issue, professionals held sway. When the item involved more personal issues of how to cope with a health issue or get quick relief, then non-professionals were preferred by most patients.

Public confidence in Internet health information has remained consistently high throughout the Web's first decade. In 2002, a Pew Internet report found that 72% of health-seekers wanted to believe all or most online health information, and 69% said they had not seen any wrong or misleading health information on the Internet.

Four years on, a Pew report recorded that three-quarters of American Internet health seekers said they checked the source and date of information "only sometimes," "hardly ever," or "never" (Fox, 2006)—this despite the fact that they were typically using the broadest of search engines, where all manner of junk sites could be returned. It appears that the identity of a website has come to provide a good clue for most users. Thus, according to a 2009 Manhattan Research report, about two thirds of Internet users thought they could tell if a medical site was from a credible source before even clicking on the search result (Marketing Charts Staff, 2009a).

Where commercial health sites are concerned, the public is on its guard. The Pew Internet report of 2002 found that almost 50% of health seekers had rejected information from a site that appeared to be promoting a product—or just sounded too commercial. For many users, heavy sponsorship is the deciding factor, even if the website gets high marks from the experts (Sillence, Briggs, Harris & Fishwick, 2007). Consumers have told researchers that they care intensely who is behind pharmaceutical and medical help sites. They fear who lurks on the Web (Nettleton, Burrows & O'Malley, 2005; Lewis, 2006; Khoo, Bolt, Babl, Jury & Goldman, 2008). Commercial sites in general are mistrusted; Princeton Survey Research Associates (2002) found that less than one third of Web users had confidence in them.

Overall, however, the Internet has eclipsed TV, radio or the printed media as the more credible source for prescription drug information (Choi & Wei-Na,

2007). One likely reason is that, whatever its problems, it hosts a substantial amount of high quality content (Huh, DeLorme & Reid, 2005; George, 2006). Another reason, no doubt, is that the Internet is like a vast library. TV and radio are just not in the same league.

Admittedly, in the rapidly morphing landscape of the World Wide Web, whatever was true yesterday may not be true tomorrow. The meteoric rise of user-generated social media has already begun to erode some of that confidence in the Internet. Thus, the 2010 Prevention Magazine Survey found that only 58% of users regarded health information on the social media as trustworthy. This was conceivably prompting—or even reflecting—a wider cooling of fervor for the Internet. The Prevention Magazine Survey for the following year actually reported a decline in online health information seeking, from a peak of 65% of adult Americans in 2010 to 55%, almost back to 2005 levels.

But a fundamental question remains: Why use the World Web Wide when your physician, your nurse or your pharmacist would be a better source of advice: they (kind of) know you, they know your history, you may even (kind of) know them—and they are real live persons. And indeed, surveys in the US, Europe and Australia show that people much prefer to have one-on-one counseling than a written text (Raynor et al., 2007).

But that is in theory. In reality, patients are not talking much to their physician about their medicines—and what time they do get is often quite limited (Morris, Tabak & Gondek, 1997; Stevenson, Cox, Britten & Dundar, 2004). According to a study of doctors starting a patient on a medicine, only a third of the patients came away with explanations of the side effects and the length of treatment, and just over half were told how to use the medication (Tarn et al., 2006).

Similarly, a majority of American pharmacists provide no counseling whatsoever to patients (Svarstad, Bultman & Mount, 2004). Pharmacists do not even generally have time to look at the patient's history on the computer screen, where they might have picked up past side effects, allergies, drug interactions and other warning signals. It actually takes an average of three to five minutes to counsel the patient properly, an expensive use of time in today's health care systems (Mayer, 2003; Mayberry, 2003).

However, even though patients may feel happier with this kind of explanation, there is a good chance that they will not recall what they have been told. Thus they will probably need written information anyway. For older Americans, written information is particularly important (Rost & Roter, 1987). According to one survey, just 58% of older patients were familiar with their dosing instructions immediately after seeing their doctor (Fletcher, Fletcher, Thomas & Hamann,

1979). Older patients are also more reluctant to ask questions or to mention that they haven't understood (Adelman, Greene & Charon, 1991).

Written information has to be crystal clear (Klein & Isaacson, 2003). However, the people who write the information are often poorly equipped to spot the problems. The prescription label *"Take two tablets by mouth twice daily"* may appear to be a simple, straightforward instruction, but some patients can take this to mean any one of the following:

Take it every 8 hours
Take it every day
Take one every 12 hours

Better directions would be *Take 2 tablets by mouth at 8 in the morning, and take 2 tablets at 9 at night.*

The perils of not having clear practical information have slowly been emerging. Of an estimated 1.5 million medication errors every year in the United States, a large proportion occur in the home—and poor labeling contributes to at least a third of all errors (Aspden, Wolcott, Bootman & Cronenwett, 2006; Berman, 2004). Poor labeling has also been named as a culprit for the widespread failure to take the medicine. Patients only take some 50% of their medication doses on average (World Health Organization, 2003), even for a chronic condition.

WHERE DRUG LEAFLETS HAVE FAILED—AND WEBSITES NEED TO SUCCEED

If online drug information is to be effective, the lessons of printed drug information must be learned.

In chapter one, we charted the sorry political saga of the humble American package insert or medication leaflet. There was a time when this was the big buzz in patient empowerment. Politicians latched on to it at the highest levels. Championed in the 1970s by Senator Edward Kennedy, drug information leaflets were proposed by the FDA in 1979 as a legal requirement for all prescription drugs. But that same year, just one day after Ronald Reagan's inauguration—as if it were the highest matter on the Administration's mind—the FDA was compelled to drop the whole idea of requiring drug information leaflets, under intense pressure from the Pharma industry. It was not until 1996 that the FDA was again permitted by Congress to take up the cause of drug information leaflets—and then, only as a recommendation. Instead, it was left to the private sector (pharmacy chains and so-called 'drug information vendors') to supply the public with the written information it now expected to receive by right.

But what actually makes for effective written drug information? Sadly, research suggests that patient leaflets have little value and that patients in many countries are paying alarmingly little attention to the instructions and precautions (Schmitt et al., 2011; Raynor, 2008).

The weaknesses of drug leaflets supplied by trusted American pharmacy chains were spelled out in a highly critical report submitted in 2001 to the FDA. Although 90% of community pharmacies were now providing computer-generated leaflets with every new prescription, consumers described the leaflets as poorly written and hard on the eyes, while experts were highly critical of the content—in particular, the precautions and the warnings. The chief culprits, according to one pharmacy systems expert, were the pharmacy chains themselves (McEvoy, 2010).

Seven years later, a second report again found the average pharmacy drug leaflet either impenetrably obscure or overly long—or both (Kimberlin & Winterstein, 2008; Winterstein, Linden, Lee, Fernandez & Kimberlin, 2010). It all prompted one of the authors to observe wryly that manuals for home appliances are generally better formatted and come with translations in several languages and troubleshooting information, even though the dangers posed by a toaster or dishwasher are minimal.

As for the FDA-approved *Medication Guides*, these have been specially commissioned by the FDA during the last few years from the manufacturers of some 200 drugs that raise a "significant public health concern," such as non-steroidal anti-inflammatory drugs (NSAIDs) and selective serotonin reuptake inhibitors (SSRIs).

Serious and potentially life-threatening problems have also been identified with these *Medication Guides*. Though required by law to be in consumer-friendly English (6th to 8th grade reading level according to FDA guidelines), they are not subject to any comprehensibility testing. Shiffman et al. (2011) tested a *Medication Guide* for comprehension by a group of subjects who had no education beyond high school. The materials were technically speaking at a 9th–10th grade reading level. However, after perusing the leaflets for 20–30 minutes and even being allowed to consult them while answering the seven questions, just 50% of the subjects on average answered the questions correctly, and 40% could not identify vital medical information about a suicide risk for teens. Bleak evidence of the deadly effect of poor health literacy on the elderly has come from a national survey published by Bostock and Steptoe (2012) in the British Medical Journal.

By 2010, the FDA was beginning to consider scrapping the *Medication Guides* and devising (or maybe 'searching for' better describes it) a standard model leaflet for all medications (Engelberg Center, 2009; 2010; Pearsall & Araojo, 2013). At a public hearing in 2010, many criticisms were voiced (e.g. Consumer Health Information Corporation, 2010).

At least 30 million American adults have 'below basic' reading skills. This is defined as meaning that, if you give them a pamphlet or a brief list of instructions, they will be hard pressed to deduce how often a person should have a specified medical test or what is permissible to drink before a medical test. They are un-likely even to be able to circle the date of a medical appointment on a hospital appointment slip. But these are not people one would expect to spot in a crowd. They may come from all manner of backgrounds; most are of average intelligence and function quite normally (Weiss & Coyne, 1997). Another 47 million have just 'basic' skills (NAAL, 2003). The pharmacy drug leaflets are clearly not designed for these 77 million Americans.

To this should be added the reading and concentration problems of the elderly (Morrell, Park & Poon, 1990). One in three over-65s in England have a hard time with basic written health information, according to a national survey published in 2012 (Bostock & Steptoe, 2012). Indeed, the problems extend to anyone having to read up on a medication in distracting circumstances—as so many parents and caregivers have to do. One study of parents trying to calculate the right dose for their child found that 56% were unable to get it right with a cough syrup (Patel, Branch & Arocha, 2002).

How far 'Medspeak' is entrenched can be seen from the warning stickers of-ten attached to drug containers. Nowhere should clarity and simplicity be more essential than on a warning sticker. But when a group of patients with an average of 5th-grade reading level were asked to explain some warning stickers, less than half could understand any of them (Wolf, Davis, Tilson, Bass & Parker, 2006). It should not require years of testing and research to come up with 'Limit your time in the sun' in place of 'You should avoid prolonged or excessive exposure to direct and/or artificial sunlight while taking this medicine' or to hit upon 'Use only on your skin' rather than 'For external use only.'

Manageable length is another key element in usability. Karen Oster of the (American) National Association of Chain Drug Stores has described the problem (Oster, 2002):

> Written information that is two or even three pages long may not be read by pa-tients because of its length, and clearly that's not a desired outcome. We understand that already about 80 percent of the information produced is greater than two pages in length.

Giving testimony to a public hearing in Washington on consumer drug informa-tion in 2003, Dr. John Coster of the National Association of Chain Drug Stores painted a byzantine picture of how pharmacists depend on a network of some 80 database and software companies to provide the information contained in patient leaflets. None of these companies, he said, was subject to regulatory oversight. Nor did pharmacists know where the information used by these companies comes from. Pharmacists sometimes even edit prescription information so it will not alarm patients. Wording of instructions varies widely between medications. As a result, another witness observed, patients have no assurance that the information is accurate, complete or consistent from one pharmacy to another (Mayberry, 2003).

Michael Wolf and colleagues have stated it bluntly: 'Lack of standards for consumer medication information places patients at risk for error' (Wolf et al., 2006).

Meanwhile, as pharmacies continue to churn out paper about the pills they dispense, millions of online Americans prefer to go to the Web for drug information—after all, this is where they now go for so much else. Indeed, there may actually be more motivation to read off the information from a laptop or smartphone than from a leaflet—in rather the same way as people are reading fiction on Kindles who might not have opened a book. Some of the leaflets may also now be found online, but the public are patronizing other sources of information altogether. That portion of America that is still largely off-line, the poor and the elderly, will also be coming online in the coming years, thanks in part to Health Care Reform (National Healthcare Quality and Disparities Reports, 2009).

WHAT ARE THE SEARCH ENGINES LISTING—AND HOW COME?

Someone recently using a laptop or smartphone to check on a medication may have gone straight to a trusted health site or perhaps typed <brand>.com. More likely, they used a search engine. Americans devote more of their Web time to e-mail and Search than to anything else.

Over four out of every five American and European web searches in 2012 were using Google (Purcell, Brenner & Rainie, 2012; Statcounter, 2013). What appears when one 'googles' a prescription drug? Of course, it depends in part on how broad or specific the search term is. In 2012, we tested a broad search, and entered the names of the 20 best-selling prescription drugs of 2010 to see what came up on the first page of results. (Users usually look no further than the first page (Morahan-Martin, 2004; Jansen & Spink, 2006).)

A clear pattern emerged:

- Commercial and for-profit sites—and mostly the same ones—dominated the first page.
- However, they never monopolized it.
- Particularly interesting, sites tied to the brand itself always appeared to be in a minority.

Here are some significant details of what we found:

Topping the page, almost always, was a link to the manufacturer's brand website. Just so you should not think that this was a natural ("organic", in tech-speak) search result, Google placed it in a lightly colored box with a tiny indicator *Ad— why this ad?* Google is paid by the manufacturer for this top spot. You are not seeing it there for any other reason than that.

The fact that the box was so faintly colored and had such a miniscule label disturbed us, just as it eventually disturbed the U.S. Federal Trade Commission. In June 2013 the FTC sent letters to 24 Internet search companies, including Google, Microsoft Corp. and Yahoo Inc, warning them (Oreskovic, 2013) that

> In recent years, paid search results have become less distinguishable as advertising, and the FTC is urging the search industry to make sure the distinction is clear.

Below the paid search results came eleven or twelve other links. The lead item, every time, was:

> *PubMed*—a government-sponsored health page.

This was by an arrangement between Google and the National Institutes of Health (Sterling, 2010).

Also present, every time, were

- *Wikipedia*
- *drugs.com*
- *rx.list*
- A second link to the manufacturer's brand website.

Other frequent presences on the first page were:

- *webmd.com*
- *medicine.net*

Besides these "regulars", there were another five or six links. These were typically some approved prescribing information, an additional brand page with safety or disease information, a commercial or user-run advice page, one or two news media items—and, for some drugs, a link to a law firm or legal action group. Spoiling or perhaps enlivening the proceedings, we often found an online pharmacy—and very occasionally, an informational YouTube clip.

What makes the cut onto the coveted first page and the prize top five spots depends on the workings of Google's top-secret PageRank algorithm—or so we are given to believe (Levy, 2010). But even when we did a broad search, Google came up with suggestions to narrow our search. At the foot of the page were six or seven links (varying from product to product) such as *side effects, dosage, generics, structure, classification, package insert, reviews, cost* and *coupons*.

And what if you 'google' a medical condition, say, *bipolar disorder, gastroesophageal reflux disease, cholesterol, type 2 diabetes* or *asthma*? Each time, again, one or two sponsored ads for a brand came first—for example, *www.bipolartreatmentinfo.com*, a feeder for *www.seroquelxr.com*. There was often also a column of sponsored links on the right of the screen.

However, the main block of results—the so-called "organic" results—was almost free of branded links. This came as a surprise. Brand agencies are known for "optimizing" their search engine rankings and conjuring their products onto the first page. Where, then, were they?

We wonder if Google has a covert policy of keeping branded links out of the "organic" results for medical conditions—and of keeping them within bounds in the "organic" results for branded drugs. A senior Google manager we spoke to could not confirm or deny that they have any particular policies in place—aside, of course, from the arrangement we referred to above (dating to June 21, 2010) to place a PubMed Health link at the top of the results.

It has been claimed that Google results depend somewhat on who you are— or more precisely, on what history of web searches Google has on file for an individual and even on where in the USA one is logging in from. Eli Pariser, in his book *The Filter Bubble*, has written that, from December 2009, "you get the result that Google's algorithm suggests is best for you in particular—and someone else may see something entirely different." (Pariser, 2011). However, we found no appreciable variations of this kind in different people's results for brand or ailment searches on Google.

WHO IS BEHIND THIS DRUG INFORMATION, AND IS IT RELIABLE?

Wherever the drug information at a high-credibility website is coming from, it has gone through a long process.

In every case, and whatever the website, the bulk of the information at an American site ultimately derives from the *Prescribing Information* as originally approved by the Food and Drug Administration. Sometimes, this is enhanced by use of peer-reviewed literature and other sources, and updated for side effect and interaction reports. In every case, as well, it will have been shortened and simplified to make it more readable. This is generally the work of pharmacologists at a large data-systems provider, a company that supplies technical information for the public.

In a few cases, use will also be made of the *Medication Guides* for patients that the FDA has commissioned from manufacturers for some 200 of the more high-risk drugs. But in any event, the bulk of the data will generally go back to the FDA-approved *Prescribing Information* (Food and Drug Administration, 2002).

Serious concerns, however, have repeatedly been voiced about some key features and components of this *Prescribing Information*—and, by implication, about the information at even the most authoritative public health portals.

Writing in the New England Journal of Medicine, Lisa Schwartz and Steven Woloshin of Dartmouth Medical School outed a little known fact: Drug labels are not written by the FDA or some other disinterested party but rather, "are written by companies, then negotiated and approved by the FDA" (Schwartz & Woloshin, 2009). The word "negotiated" should raise eyebrows. Schwartz and Woloshin went on to cite cases, publicly available in the FDA review documents for a drug application, in which some risks of a drug or its marginal effectiveness were signaled by the reviewers—and yet, peculiarly, never got a mention in the *Prescribing Information*. Three drugs they cite are Zometa (zoledronic acid), Lunesta (eszopiclone), and Rozerem (ramelteon). As they put it, rather coyly:

> In many cases, information gets lost between FDA review and the approved label. Sometimes, what gets lost is data on harms [...] sometimes, efficacy data get lost.

In 2006, in fact, the FDA had issued guidance to improve the reporting of trial results in the prescribing information. This emphasized the importance of the data on effectiveness. Subsequently, the information for Lunesta and Rozerem was updated, in 2008 and 2009—a perfect opportunity for data on their effectiveness to be included. But this did not happen.

Communicative concerns of a different kind were raised in 2002 at an FDA hearing by an information manager at First DataBank, one of the largest data providers to retail pharmacies. There is, he argued, too much emphasis on the risks of drugs in the FDA-approved *Medication Guides* and *Prescribing Information*. Patients reading these sources on their own, without a doctor to advise them and to place the risks in proper perspective, could easily be spooked.

For example, these patients, upon reading of the risk of death due to rhabdomyolysis from the cholesterol lowering statin drugs, may frequently refuse to take the medication. Even worse, patients are reported to be giving up on their medication in over 40% of cases (Food and Drug Administration, 2002).

It should be borne in mind that these concerns apply to all American prescription drug labeling, whether on the World Wide Web or in printed form.

Amid all the variety we will find on the drug sites we inspect, the same general culture of 'Medspeak' and economy with the truth prevails.

WHEN IS A WEBSITE USER-FRIENDLY?

Trust is one thing, usability another. How much can be learnt from a text is largely a matter of how readable it is: in its language and organization of content, its layout and legibility, and its credibility.

Usability of risk information, such as product warnings, road signs and patient leaflets, has long been of concern to safety organizations and to consumer groups. But the Internet has totally changed the playing field. A website is fundamentally unlike other forms of communication, and poses unique problems to its readers (Nielsen, 2000; Glinert, 2001; Lynch & Horton, 1999).

First: There Is No Intuitive Route Through a Website

Anyone still used to reading books or brochures or newspapers in hard copy will understand what it means to have an intuitive reading route to follow. Websites, however, have no obvious "next page" and no obvious point of closure. Often, there isn't even a clear starting point on a home page. Instead, websites are designed to be "hypermodal" (Lemke, 2002), meaning that they are constructed around a deliberately unordered series of links.

One is therefore constantly compelled to make navigation choices. If the website provides a site map—and few do—it will normally be hidden away with some other tiny links at the foot of a page. Tables of contents are even rarer. The result is a kind of maze. An analysis of 500 corporate websites in 2006 found that

> Just 10% used a breadcrumb trail showing the path back to home page
> 23% had a site search capacity
> 14% offered a FAQ or Help option

Link navigation issues were cited as the second worst design mistake of 2005 by readers of the Jakob Nielsen newsletter (Nielsen, 2005a).

User-friendly link labels could be a user's lifeline—but research has found that the first two or three words are commonly all that gets noticed, owing in part to the bizarre scanning habits that we seem to practice on the Web (Nielsen, 2009). So we often find ourselves at the wrong site, with the new problem of tracing our way back. It is not surprising that people seldom venture beyond the first page of a site (Morahan-Martin, 2004).

This is all particularly hard on older users. They need more help with orientation and many of them are simply less at home on the Web. Although an AARP survey in 2010 found that almost half of adults aged 50 to 64 felt a competence with the Internet (Koppen, 2010), this figure falls off rapidly with older people. Navigability has been cited by Internet users over 50 as their top problem with using the Internet. But users of any age are cognitively challenged by website design, whether they know it or not: It seriously diminishes their capacity and their willingness to focus. A British Department of Health report has found that the average time a user spends viewing a page is just 10–12 seconds (Nicholas, Huntington & Williams, 2004).

Second: The Overall Thrust of a Website Is Hard to Judge

An editing defect that seems to be endemic to company drug websites is *patchworking*: the practice of building pages out of shreds and patches, seemingly recycled from some other place—with little sign of an overall guiding hand.

Compounding the problem, a website—unlike a book or a pamphlet—has no obvious place to look at for a summary or a parting message. Even TV and radio commercials, for all their razzmatazz, generally conclude on a slogan, due to the fact that they are listened to in real time. Viewing a web page, one may be drawn to a banner text, but this will not be a "punch line".

Third: We Do Not "Read" an Individual Web Page in the Way We Read a Printed Page

Psychologists have found that we do not expect a web page to be organized with the same logic as a printed page. Instead, we expect a "disconnect of matter". Sometimes, in fact, we circle around the text, performing "Web rings". This is due in part to the way in which the mind views a computer page (Kaplan, 2000; Lemke, 2002; Warnick, 2006).

These habits have been reinforced by web page designers, who are often more eager to stimulate than to inform. Page editors for their part are quite content with the practice of "patchworking" all manner of sources, to which we just alluded.

At the best of times, a page of computer text itself is hard to read. Indeed, there is evidence that high-literate users generally scan rather than read computer screen text. They commonly scan in an F-pattern, i.e. plowing the upper content bloc (typically the first two paragraphs), then a shorter bloc below it, and then scanning down the left side of the page. Remarkably, even high-literate users generally read no more than 20–25% of the text on a visit to a page (Nielsen, 1997a; 2006; 2008).

The alternative, making a print-out of a set of pages, is a tiresome chore. There is also evidence that many online health seekers are looking for easy-to-print materials to give to family or friends (Hesse et al., 2005).

Fourth: Content Keeps Changing—Without Warning

Content is liable to change or vanish from one visit to the next, with no clue as to what has changed. Often, there isn't even an indication of when the page or website was last updated—and if there is, it will be tucked away at the very foot of the page. What compounds the confusion is that readers tend to work on the assumption that nothing has changed.

Fifth: Own-Site Search Boxes Are a Problem to Use

At some time, most users will have tried typing a word or two into a site's own search box. But here, again, caution is advised. Search engines vary in how they handle hyphens, plurals and the like—as well as in how they prioritize the results (Nielsen, 2010).

Sixth: Designers Seem to Relish Tiny Print

Designers often use fonts of a size that may just be acceptable on the printed page but not on the computer screen. Tiny fonts were nominated as by far the worst design mistake of 2005 by readers of the Jakob Nielsen newsletter (Nielsen, 2005a).

Finally: The Mother of All Problems

A thread that runs through all the problems just enumerated is that things are not what they seem. In so many ways, the Web environment is a look-alike of the books, papers and pamphlets that American adults have been raised on. But the differences are immense. Of all the problems they face in comprehending a dizzily changing world, none is greater than to assume that they do comprehend it.

To quote Nielsen himself:

> Consistency is one of the most powerful usability principles. The more users' expectations prove right, the more they will feel in control of the system and the more they will like it. (Nielsen, 2010)

BROADER PROBLEMS WITH THE WORLD WIDE WEB

The World Wide Web poses other, broader challenges. One is an unhealthy dependency on search engines—currently, above all, on Google. Google or any other general search engine nets an unpredictable catch of nuggets and junk. Few users have the slightest idea what complex computer programs and financial sponsorship deals the people behind the search engines have devised to determine what sites rise to the top—and by what means, fair and foul, companies try to outsmart them. Alarmingly, Web searchers seldom look beyond the first page of results (Morahan-Martin, 2004). It would not be an overstatement to say that our daily lives are increasingly at the mercy of the search engine. As Alexander Halavais has argued in his book *Search Engine Society*, search engines have even changed the way people marshal their thoughts about the world (Halavais, 2008).

Some of the sites we are going to examine are known to many users, and they will arrive there of their own accord. But how they get to some of the other sites is a matter of how and whether a search engine takes them there.

It is difficult, therefore, to agree with the CEO of one leading health information platform, claiming to reach over 100 million consumers a year, who exults:

Consumers are empowered by choice, and the user—not the information provider—controls how, what and when content is received. (Cunnion, 2010).

Far from it. Consumers have very little say in what the search engines serve up on a first page of search results, nor in how the content they see is cooked and garnished. The myth of the empowered consumer presiding over incoming information is the marketer's latest attempt—in a never-ending game of cat and mouse—to appear on the side of the angels.

A second challenge is an ever-shorter attention span, which has been linked experimentally to reading off the screen and surfing the Web. In the words of Nicholas Carr, the author of *The Shallows: What the Internet Is Doing to Our Brains* (2008):

What the Net seems to be doing is chipping away at my capacity for concentration and contemplation.

No doubt, the constantly increasing speed of gadgetry plays its part. All of this makes it imperative that any medical information we read at a website is maximally clear and "readable".

PROTECTING THE VULNERABLE: AMERICAN SENIORS
AND THE LESS LITERATE

Working the Web seems to be particularly hard on seniors. Jakob Nielsen tested seniors on four fact-based Web tasks and found a 53% success rate—compared with 78% for a comparable group aged 21–55. The seniors also took overall 70% longer on the tasks (Nielsen, 2002). Impaired eyesight or hand movement will, naturally, add to the problems.

As for the 40% of American Internet users with a grade reading level below 9th grade, this massive demographic group is frequently termed "the less literate" (Nielsen, 2005b). They are thought to view websites quite differently: Rather than scan to identify key information, they read word for word. Scrolling disorients them. So do busy Web pages and graphics. Spelling a search term is a further headache (Zarcadoolas, Blanco, Boyer & Pleasant, 2002; Nielsen, 2005b).

But there is hope in simplicity. Pfizer Inc., as part of a long-term project to promote health literacy, funded a study of how the less-literate search the Web for health information (Vernon, Trujillo, Rosenbaum & DeBuono, 2007). A less-literate group and a higher-literacy group were given seven fact-based Web tasks to perform at a major Pharma product site, designed by a respected agency. On the one hand, the less-literate group had a 46% success rate, as against 68% for the higher-literacy group. On the other, this rose to an 82% success rate when the site was simplified—simply by placing the most important information at the top of the page, listing the main choices in a menu, and the like. Unfortunately, many web designers do not seem to be concerned.

As smartphones, tablets and social media become second nature, virtually all Americans will develop some comfort level with the Internet, and perhaps with the health Web (Lewis, 2006; Nettleton et al., 2005).

However, a systemic problem remains, not with patients but with the professionals who are supposed to care about them: The American health care system appears to be chronically incapable of providing readable information to at least 50% of Americans. The conclusion of the Pfizer report (2007) cited earlier bears repeating:

> At virtually every point along the healthcare services spectrum, the healthcare system behaves in a way that requires patients to read and understand important healthcare information. This information is dense, technical, and has jargon-filled language. Examples include completing health insurance applications, reading signs in hospitals and clinics about where to go and where to sign in, and following written and oral instructions in brochures and pamphlets, as well as prescription medication directions.

Government interest in literacy in general is very recent: The first America-wide survey of adult literacy, The National Adult Literacy Survey, was only completed in 1992 and the first British survey in 1997. Results showed that a sizable minority lacked a basic everyday functional literacy. But that is nothing compared with the need to understand complex health information, which is what is expected for *health* literacy. Nearly half of all American adults have difficulty coping with commonly encountered health literature, such as medical instructions, insurance and consent forms or privacy notices, according to the first major survey of health literacy, by the Institute of Medicine (Nielsen-Bohlman, Panzer & Kindig, 2004) and in the work of Paasche-Orlow, Parker, Gazmararian, Nielsen-Bohlman & Rudd (2005). One can hardly blame schools or students—the Institute of Medicine makes the chilling observation that

> even people with strong literacy skills may have trouble obtaining, understanding, and using complex health information […] a science teacher may not understand information sent by a doctor about a brain function test; and an accountant may not know when to get a mammogram.

Low numeracy is just as serious and widespread a problem for Americans (Peters, Hibbard, Slovic & Dieckmann, 2007). Numeracy spans "simple" arithmetic tasks such as figuring out how many 5 mg pills you need for a 30 mg dose and probabilistic concepts like the risks of kidney failure from a medication. Frequencies can create a special kind of fog: For many Americans, one out of 10 does not mean the same thing as 10% (Schapira, Nattinger & McHorney, 2001). The Institute of Medicine's report of 2004 concluded that nearly half of all American adults have difficulty understanding and acting upon health information involving the most basic of mathematical skills (Nielsen-Bohlman et al., 2004). In some cases, perhaps, there is an advantage in words instead of numbers—"a small number of, rarely, very common". But increased simplicity for some people is increased vagueness for others (Schwartz, Woloshin, Black & Welch, 1997). The health system has only just begun to grapple with low numeracy.

Even in the one area of health communication that does preoccupy American lawmakers, direct-to-consumer advertising, there is little research on the effect on vulnerable groups: the elderly, children, racial and ethnic minority communities. The FDA had to admit this in a report to Congress on drug advertising and the vulnerable (Report to Congress, 2009).

Every aspect of low literacy and numeracy that bedevils American society is being magnified by the World Wide Web. A consensual adoption of best practices has been proposed by leaders in the field (Lynch & Horton, 1999; Nielsen, 2000; Nielsen, 2007–2010), but Web designers have shown little inclination to listen, and many Pharma brand managers do not appear to appreciate two simple facts that we underlined earlier: two of the chief factors in creating trust in a website are coherent organization and navigability.

With all these communicative challenges, the consumer seeking information on prescription drugs is ill-equipped to deal with what is the most striking characteristic of brand drug sites: the fuzzy mix of promotion and information. We will address this presently.

TEXT, CONTEXT, MESSAGE

A plethora of factors contribute to the effect of a message, as has belatedly begun to be recognized (Halliday, 1978; Hymes, 1964; Levinson, 1979). Here are some of the more obvious, with a few examples in parentheses:

- Who is sending it?
  (Age, gender, ethnicity, other social status? Are the author and the sender the same person?)
- What form does the message take?
  (Is it handwritten, print, Web-based, direct word, recorded? And what grammar, choice of words, style, sounds, rhythms, format, font etc? How explicit is it?)
- What does the message mean?
  (What do the words in themselves mean? What is the sender getting at?)
- What is the goal of the interchange?
  (To educate? to joke? To pass the time of day? To sell something?)
- What is the frame of the message—the accompanying texts, images, music and so on? What type of text is this? What type of situation?
  (Are the words part of an ad? a patient leaflet? a consult?)
- What is the relationship of sender and recipient?
  (friends? colleagues? nurse-patient? pleasant? hostile?)
- Who is the recipient?
  (a specific person or group? anyone who's out there?)
- What does the recipient bring to the encounter?
  (attitude, beliefs, background knowledge, involvement, expectations)

Some of these questions are the province of linguists, some of psychologists, sociologists and anthropologists, and many belong to communications analysis and the study of rhetoric. As we investigate the presentation of prescription drugs on the Web, we will be keeping some of these factors in mind—focusing on language, context, and rhetoric.

Communication is about so much more than the set of standards laid down by the FDA in its 2006 *Guidance Document on Useful Written Consumer Medication Information.* The experts who were then commissioned to evaluate pharmacy consumer sheets laid down the following criteria: The information must include (Kimberlin & Winterstein, 2008):

1. drug names and indications for use
2. contraindications and what to do if applicable
3. specific directions about how to use, monitor, and get most benefit
4. specific precautions and how to avoid harm while using it
5. symptoms of serious or frequent adverse reactions and what to do
6. general information and encouragement to ask questions

It must also be

7. scientifically accurate, unbiased, and up-to-date
8. easily comprehensible and legible

The consumers who joined them in the evaluation had to rate the leaflets for print size and quality, spacing, organization, length, clarity, helpfulness, completeness, ease of finding important information.

But at the same time, there may be space limitations—as with the holy grail of patient leaflets, the one-page hand-out. Experts gathered in 2011 at the Brookings Institution spoke of different possible focuses: an alert to the risks, a reference sheet to supplement what the doctor said, and a set of instructions for use. Of course, the Internet (like the Physicians' Desk Reference) allows for everything—in theory—but even there the issue remains: How and where to focus users' attention and how to explain the content (Engelberg Center, 2009).

We can take a still broader perspective: What kind of attention or consideration does one give a message, and why? If leaflets in our "throw-away" culture tend to be looked upon as junk, is there anything we can do to get them more attention when they're on the Web?

In our case, what really *is* an Internet site, how do users relate to it, and how do they understand it?

WHAT THE PUBLIC LOOKS FOR IN A DRUG WEBSITE—AND WHAT WE CHECKED FOR

The number of U.S. sites where one can go for drug information is hard to estimate. There are brand sites, Facebook and Twitter and other social media pages, new mobile apps opening up every day—and of course, medical information sites and health portals.

Dedicated medical information sites and portals number in the three figures, and are constantly reproducing and morphing. Many general portals and encyclopedias, such as yahoo.com, Wikipedia and about.com, also have medical-related sections. Some portals are expert-run (e.g. PubMed Health), others are run by patients (e.g. Askapatient).

The degree of commercialism varies from site to site, even from page to page. Some medical sites are non-commercial, notably PubMed Health and Wikipedia. Some, such as Good Health Media, receive drug manufacturer sponsorship discreetly. Most, however, pay varying degrees of homage to the names of the drug manufacturers sponsoring them. Here is not the place to discuss what privileged health information about individuals and groups these sites secretly pass on to their sponsors. Rather, we are concerned with the information these sites openly provide to the public.

We have already spoken of the risks and benefits to consumers of the rampant commercialism that surrounds so much drug information. The World Health Organization has described drug promotion as "an inherent conflict of interest between the legitimate business goals of manufacturers and the social, medical and economic needs of providers and the public" (World Health Organization, 2013). We also described the safeguards set in place by regulators—but we showed how these have been found wanting. The U.S. Federal Trade Commission requires that "Advertising must be truthful and not misleading"—yet much drug advertising is indeed misleading. The FDA requires that drug advertising maintain a strict balance between risk and benefit information—yet much drug information involves advertising that violates this balance.

Among well-known non-brand medical sites with a focus on drugs are:

PubMed Health
MedlinePlus
Drugsaz.about.com (a component of about.com)
WebMD.com and its affiliates: Medicinenet.com and Rxlist.com
Mayoclinic.com
Drugs.com
Localhealth.com
Walgreens.com
Patientslikeme.com
RateADrug.com
Askapatient.com
CrazyMeds.us
Peoplespharmacy.com
Mediguard.org

What sort of health care site do Americans prefer? A PricewaterhouseCoopers survey (2010) found a big difference in first preferences. The survey divided healthcare sites into four kinds:

1. information companies and TV-related sites such as WebMD, iVillage, Dr. Oz and The Doctors
2. health services and manufacturers such as the Mayo Clinic and Johnson & Johnson
3. government organizations such as the FDA and the Centers for Disease Control and Prevention
4. consumer-driven organizations such as Daily Strength, PatientsLikeMe and Angie's List

Fifty-six percent of American consumers said that they are most likely to use information companies and TV-related sites. The rest were split three ways, almost evenly: Around 16% said that their first choice was the sites of health services and manufacturers, while another 16% preferred government organizations. Just 12% listed as first choice consumer-driven organizations.

Revealingly, however, the Prevention Magazine survey of 2011 reported that, while not the majority *first* choice, drug product brand sites were being visited by no less than 49% of those seeking prescription drug information online, and indeed 44% of seekers said they found them very useful (Rodale, 2011). While the numbers of those visiting all particular arthritis drug sites in late 2010 were less than 5% of those who visit a general arthritis or health site, those actually prescribed an arthritis drug will quite likely visit its brand.com pages. Thus, between August 2010 and August 2011, celebrex.com had 108,000 unique visits per month, while seroquelxr.com, crestor.com and lipitor.com had 174,000, 153,000 and 198,000 visits, respectively (Pharmaceutical Marketing, 2011).

Little else is public knowledge about what draws people to what sort of site, but it is reasonable to assume that the combination of medical expertise, media glitz and broader interest is what draws those 56% of consumers to WebMD or Dr. Oz. Clearly, also, the attractions of hearing from fellow consumers sometimes count for less than medical expertise. As the 2011 Pew Report on Health in the Social Media put it (Fox, 2011):

> When the item involved technical issues related to a health issue, professionals held sway. When the item involved more personal issues of how to cope with a health issue or get quick relief, then non-professionals were preferred by most patients.

Nor is much known about *how* people find a site. Many probably arrive by a search engine. This can influence what sort of site they visit. In a Google search for a condition, the first page of results in August 2011 will have been a mix of health portals and brand sites. We searched for "cholesterol, depression, hypertension, diabetes". At the top, in each case, were two or three sponsored links—though some users may not realize that they are sponsored—and in nine out of eleven cases they brought us to a brand site, e.g. zetia.com, seroquel.com, victoza.com. Thus, users may often be arriving at a manufacturer's brand site without wishing to. More on this later.

For our evaluations, we took samples at all four sorts of site that we just listed, but in the following order (with "health services and manufacturers" split into two, #3 and 4 below):

1. government-sponsored organizations:
   PubMed
2. Information companies and TV-related sites:
   about.com, WebMD, drugs.com
3. health services:
   Mayoclinic, Walgreens
4. manufacturers' brand sites
5. consumer-driven organizations (social media): PatientsLikeMe, YouTube, Wikipedia

We did not look at blogs or narrow forums, although this is where specific drugs are mostly talked about, in very idiosyncratic and often disparaging ways, in the social media. Nor did we explore relatively little used government-sponsored sources such as the downloadable *Medication Guides* at the FDA's website. Our focus was on broad reference sites with a large following.

On our visits, we paid close attention to four things:

1. oversight and responsibility
2. content
3. organization
4. language

Herein lies the core of effective communication of information.

CHAPTER THREE

Government-Sponsored Organizations

PubMed Health—Why Does It Top the List?

WHAT IS PUBMED HEALTH?

If you performed a Google search in the U.S. for a prescription drug in 2013, your #1 result—after any sponsored links—was probably PubMed Health.

This would not always have been the case. Up until June 2010 the top result would usually have been a site belonging to the company who produced the product. But then, on June 21, 2010, Google discreetly adjusted its algorithm for searches conducted in the U.S., making PubMed Health #1.

This would appear to have been a development in the public interest. PubMed Health is a non-commercial, government-funded database, hosted at the National Institutes of Health (www.nlm.nih.gov). The data are the work of the American Society of Health-System Pharmacists (Ricketts, 2010; Sterling, 2010; McEvoy, 2012). If you visit the PubMed Health *about.us* page, you learn that PubMed Health provides consumers with "up-to-date information on diseases, conditions, injuries, drugs, supplements, treatment options, and healthy living, with a special focus on comparative effectiveness research from institutions around the world."

Encouragingly, the site ranked #274 in popularity for American visitors—not far off the #198 achieved by WebMD (Alexa, 2011).

We visited PubMed Health via its home page and via some top Google results linking to it. We looked at three drugs—Lipitor, Betaseron and Humira—to evaluate the information at PubMed. Here are some of our findings:

WHO'S IN CHARGE?

We had to scroll down to the foot of the page to discover that oversight is in the hands of:

> The American Society of Health-Systems Pharmacists and the National Center for Biotechnological Information, US National Library of Medicine.

You could learn more about PubMed by clicking on a small link *About PubMed Health* at the top of the page. This was all reassuring.

While adequate, it would help less able users if this information were displayed prominently at the top of the page.

WHAT DOES PUBMED TELL YOU?

On the face of it, PubMed Health gives consumers all they probably need to know. Here are the 12 topics we found listed:

- Why is this medication prescribed?
- How should this medicine be used?
- Other uses for this medicine
- What special precautions should I follow?
- What special dietary instructions should I follow?
- What should I do if I forget a dose?
- What side effects can this medication cause?
- What storage conditions are needed for this medicine?
- In case of emergency/overdose
- What other information should I know?
- Brand names
- Brand names of combination products

Missing, however, was any indication about **how effective** the drug really is. How does it compare with taking a placebo? How does it compare with other drugs of its class? How does effectiveness vary for different groups of Americans?

HOW WELL IS PUBMED ORGANIZED?

With PubMed, searching for what we wanted looked invitingly simple. We were spared always having to click our way into the website—thanks to the row of sub-links running under the link itself:

Side effects   *How to take*   *Precautions*   *Dietary Instructions*   *Missed a dose*

None of the other 12 Google results for Lipitor (including lipitor.com, drugs.com and webmd.com) provided such immediate signposts.

RECOMMENDATION: Website designers should ensure that a sub-list of "signpost" links of the type *Side effects/How to take/Precautions* appear with every result.

Actionable items were not adequately organized. On the one hand, side effects were distinctly divided between **non-urgent and urgent**, and **bulleted** clearly. On the other hand, the **emergency number** for overdoses etc. was buried among a mass of information. Nor did the site authors allot separate space for things **requiring action** at different times: (a) when taking the medication and (b) when following up with the doctor—such as reporting any side effects and listing any medicines and health products being taken.

RECOMMENDATION: All *actionable items* while on the medication or before a follow-up with the doctor should be grouped prominently.

RECOMMENDATION: The emergency number should be displayed prominently at the top of the page and in the links accompanying the site description on the browser results.

HOW WELL IS PUBMED WRITTEN?

It is no use providing authoritative facts if sentences and paragraphs are **long and unwieldy**. Here is a paragraph from the Lipitor page that could do with some slimming and simplification:

Atorvastatin is used along with diet, exercise, and weight-loss to reduce the risk of heart attack and stroke and to decrease the chance that heart surgery will be needed in people who have heart disease or who are at risk of developing heart disease. Atorvastatin is also used to decrease the amount of cholesterol (a fat-like substance) and other fatty substances in the blood. This will decrease the risk of stroke, heart attack, and other heart diseases because when there are high levels of cholesterol and other fats in the blood, these substances may build up along the walls of the blood vessels and decrease or block blood flow to the heart. Atorvastatin is in a class of medications called HMG-CoA reductase inhibitors (statins). It works by slowing the production of cholesterol in the body.

Nor is it any use providing easy-to-read sentences if whole paragraphs **lack coherence.** Too often, we found **duplicated and disorderly information.** The PubMed text for Atorvastatin contrasted poorly with Pfizer's *Important Facts* for Lipitor:

> Lipitor is a prescription medicine. Along with diet and exercise, it lowers "bad" cholesterol in your blood. It can also raise "good" cholesterol (HDL-C).
>
> Lipitor can lower the risk of heart attack, stroke, certain types of heart surgery, and chest pain in patients who have heart disease or risk factors for heart disease such as: age, smoking, high blood pressure, low HDC-L, family history of early heart disease.
>
> Lipitor can lower the risk of heart attack or stroke in patients with diabetes and risk factors such as diabetic eye or kidney problems, smoking, or high blood pressure.

There were also two perplexing factual differences in the content of PubMed and the Pfizer brief summary:

a. At PubMed, the efficacy of Atorvastatin is portrayed as a certainty. In Pfizer, the efficacy of Lipitor is portrayed as an unquantified possibility ('can lower')
b. At Pfizer, the efficacy of Lipitor is limited to certain types of patient.

RECOMMENDATION: Authoritative content should be reviewed as carefully for style and coherence as for scientific accuracy.

PubMed has a lot to offer, and we applaud the fact that Google decided to rank it #1 for American searchers rather than any of the for-profit sites, but what we saw left much to be done to render content actionable and to deserve that #1.

We now cross gingerly from the Government infosphere, where commercial interests are reined in and kept carefully out of sight, into another dimension in which information and education seem to hold sway—but where commercial interests have a clear stake: Information companies and TV-related health sites.

CHAPTER FOUR

Information Companies and TV-Related Sites

About.com (including drugsaz.about.com), WebMD.com (including medicinenet.com), Drugs.com

About.com has, at time of writing, the distinction of being the third most visited general reference site in the U.S. and ranks # 38 of American sites (#87 globally) according to Alexa.com (Alexa, 2013) and #19 according to Quantcast.com (Quantcast, 2013).

A noteworthy feature of about.com are its "guides", appointed by about.com as lay "experts"—folks like you and me who are meant to have the experiences and knowledge to guide you comfortably through the subject. At drugsaz.about.com and *<condition>*.about.com are two sections of about.com that offer original articles on prescription drugs, created by "guides" of this type. They also contain third party content.

When we paid our first call on about.com, we expected it would be a brief one. About.com has a well-deserved reputation for clear and concise articles and sensible organization. But what we found impelled us to conduct a close inspection of three prescription drugs—AcipHex, Betaseron and Humira—and to recommend several improvements.

WHO'S IN CHARGE?

This may be the third most visited general reference site in the U.S., but one may still want to know: Who is in charge? Who ensures that all the information is correct? And who is responsible if it is not?

But figuring out just who was medically in charge at about.com was a challenge. First, we had to spot a tiny *Ethics Policy* link. This led us to the following:

> **Medical Review Process:** All original Articles are created by expert Guides and are reviewed by our medical review board prior to publication. All Third Party Content is obtained from third-party providers whose editorial processes *have been evaluated and deemed acceptable.* Sources of third-party content *include*: government agencies, not-for-profit foundations, and professional medical publishers of health information. *(our italics)*

This raises several questions: "evaluated" by whom? (the Medical Review Board?) and "acceptable" by what criteria? Is "third party content" indicated as such and its source indicated? (The pages for AcipHex, for example, gave no source or authorship.) What is about.com policy on off-label uses? The word "include" begs the question: What other kind of third party sources are being used—for-profit sources?

Another puzzle awaited us when we followed the *medical review board* link at the paragraph just quoted. This brought us to a page entitled *About.com Medical Review Board*, which stated:

> All About.com content focusing on diseases, conditions or containing health claims is reviewed by a team of board certified physicians and certified health professionals from leading institutions. The Medical Review Board was formed in October 2006 and all content created from that date forward has been closely reviewed for medical accuracy and consistency with source material.

We pondered the words "*About.com content focusing on diseases, conditions or containing health claims*". Does this include all drug information—or could that be Third Party Content? And again: By what criteria are some topics drawn from Third Party Content, and how is the distinction indicated? The home page could have been more transparent about these issues.

We now turn to the "guides", about.com's pride and joy. Who and what are they? The website stated (*Guide Selection*) that guides shall practice objectivity and shall disclose any conflict of interest. They shall also be experts: "Guides engaged by About.com, are real people with passion and expertise in their fields." We did, at least, find that the guides are identified by name—for what it's worth.

However, writing in the magazine *Information Today*, Mick O'Leary has put it rather differently (O'Leary, 2011).

> About.com's articles are written and maintained by about 800 freelance writers, or Guides in About.com terminology, who work independently and are paid a mixture of

salary and commission. Many Guides have academic or professional credentials, while others are knowledgeable amateurs. All are generally up to the task, both for subject knowledge and the ability to write clearly and directly. In addition, full-time editors oversee their work.

Are the guides in about.com's medications section "knowledgeable amateurs"? And if they are, what kind of oversight do those "full-time editors" provide? About.com's vast user pool should be asking some questions.

In any event, if the medication guides do in many cases have "academic or professional credentials", this would seemingly put about.com in a very different league than Wikipedia. Wikipedia claims to prefer mass amateur knowledge over scholarly expertise (although in practice this is not always so—see our profile of Wikipedia).

WHAT DOES ABOUT.COM TELL YOU?

This is the kind of drug information we found for a particular drug:

Generic name and brand names—including competitors
A statement 'This medication is available by prescription only.'
Why the drug is prescribed
Special precautions
Missing a dose
Side effects
Storage
Sources (CDER Consumer Drug Information Sheet, FDA Approval)

As with PubMed Health (see chapter 3), there was no indication of how effective the drug really is.

HOW WELL IS ABOUT.COM ORGANIZED?

We actually found not one but three jumping-off platforms at about.com for prescription drugs:

a. the about.com home page
b. drugsaz.about.com
c. <condition>.about.com (e.g. heartburn.about.com)

There is nothing wrong with that—except that the content at each of these platforms was bewilderingly different. In fact, we got the feeling that three quite different hands had been at work. Articles at drugsaz.about.com were anonymous, while articles at <condition>.about.com were authored by various "guides". Curiously, the content there had a technical rather than patient-friendly feel. But more worryingly, each platform seemed to lack some essential information that the other offered—and there was nothing to direct the user from one to the other.

The problem was at its most acute with actionable items:

(a) Urgent vs. Non-Urgent Action on Side Effects

At drugsaz.about.com we found a proper distinction between

"Side effects that you should report to your doctor or health care professional as soon as possible"

and

"Side effects that usually do not require medical attention (report to your doctor or health care professional if they continue or are bothersome)"

For example, for Humira, it listed for urgent side effects:

allergic reactions like skin rash, itching or hives, swelling of the face, lips, or tongue
breathing problems
changes in vision
chest pain
fever, chills, or any other sign of infection
numbness or tingling
swelling of the ankles
unusual bleeding or bruising
unusually weak or tired

Yet at the corresponding <condition>.about.com pages, no such distinction was made. Thus, at arthritis.about.com it simply stated, with no suggestion of urgency:

Common side effects associated with Humira include:

mild injection site reaction
rash
headache
stomach upset or nausea
pneumonia

(b) Other Important Side Effect Actions

Similarly, the AcipHex and Betaseron pages at drugsaz.about.com gave this important advice:

- This list may not describe all possible side effects.
- You may report side effects to FDA at 1-800-FDA-1088.

And the AcipHex page added:

- It can take several days before your stomach pain gets better. Check with your doctor or health care professional if your condition does not start to get better, or if it gets worse.

But the AcipHex pages at heartburn.about.com and the Betaseron pages at ms.about.com gave no such advice.

(c) Conditions You Must Report to Your Doctor

At the Humira pages at drugsaz.about.com > *Overview*, a dozen conditions were listed under "Your health care provider needs to know…" But at arthritis.about.com (*The Facts of Humira*), only a few of these were listed, and at psoriasis.about.com (*Humira (Adalimumab)*) none at all.

(d) Interactions

At drugsaz.about.com, the AcipHex pages gave a page of interactions—as well as how to take AcipHex and what to do for an overdose. None of this appeared at heartburn.about.com.

The Betaseron pages at drugsaz.about.com mentioned interaction with Zidovudine, AZT. Yet the Betaseron pages at ms.about.com state: "Not contraindicated for use with any drug".

The Humira pages at drugsaz.about.com > *Interactions* mentioned seven interactions—but arthritis.about.com only mentioned "Other biologic DMARDs" and psoriasis.about.com none at all.

INFORMATION AND PROMOTION SHOULDN'T MIX

Advertising is allowed on about.com, but company policy requires strict separation:

All advertising content is clearly distinguished from the editorial content by the following labels: advertisement, sponsored links, ads.

Advertising Policy

Labeling the ads as such is helpful, but that is surely inadequate. Editorial content often snaked about the ads and jostled with other links, failing to convey a clear organizational principle or "narrative". Visitors in a hurry need a clear path; so too, anyone who comes to about.com saying "Educate me".

Someone searching for a particular drug at the about.com home page should not first have to encounter three sponsored links—which led not to about.com pages but instead to brand.com brand sites, Walmart prescriptions sites and the like. This is not what one should expect from an information portal, let alone one with the reputation of about.com.

> RECOMMENDATION: The about.com medical content is in need of a tighter presentational and organizational hand.

> RECOMMENDATION: Emergency information (serious side effects, overdoses) should be highlighted and easy to locate.

WEBMD.COM

In 2011, WebMD was described by the Pew Internet and American Life Project as "one of the top health websites" (Fox, 2011), while the Associated Press was calling it "by far the leading health portal in the country" (Associated Press, 2011)—with 86.4 million visitors per month in the United States. Alexa.com ranked it #125 in the U.S. and Quantcast.com #52 (estimated) on July 23, 2013.

A Headache for WebMD

In late February 2010, an ominous letter landed on the desk of WebMD Health Corporation's chief executive officer. It came from Senator Chuck Grassley (Iowa), Ranking Member of the U.S. Senate Committee on Finance. Sen. Grassley had previously exposed several physicians in academia for taking large payments from companies with a direct financial stake in their research. The third paragraph of his letter to WebMD stated:

> Recently, it was brought to my attention that WebMD Health Corporation (WebMD) is running a depression screening advertisement on television. This advertisement encourages the viewer to take a screening test sponsored by Eli Lilly on WebMD's website. I am concerned about the independence (sic) between WebMD and industry since many people access WebMD seeing it as an independent, objective medical resource.

The senator went on to request all contracts and communications with pharmaceutical companies regarding the creation of the WebMD depression screening test, and an accounting of industry funding to WebMD Health Corporation. Thus was launched an investigation into WebMD's commercial relationship with the drug manufacturer Eli Lilly.

A few days later, the blog *bnet.com* cast some more light on WebMD's Depression Test, sponsored by Eli Lilly, maker of the antidepressant Cymbalta (Edwards, 2010a):

> Even if you answer "no" to *all* of the 10 questions (which are all framed so that the "yes" answer indicates depressed behavior) you still get this response:

> *Lower Risk: You may be at risk for major depression*

The blog put it bluntly: "it is rigged." Within days, WebMD had gently scaled down the response you got for answering "no" to 0–4 questions (Edwards, 2010b):

> Lower Risk
> You replied that you are feeling four or fewer of the common symptoms of depression. In general, people experiencing depression have five or more common symptoms of the condition. But every individual is unique. If you are concerned about depression, talk with your doctor.

Further controversy flared in February 2011 when the New York Times Magazine ran an op-ed by their columnist Virginia Heffernan (of "The Medium") condemning WebMD as "permeated with pseudo-medical and subtle misinformation" (Heffernan, 2011). One of Heffernan's complaints was about "the way WebMD frames health information commercially"—a problem that we are about to address in rather more depth and detail. She also faulted WebMD for having "the junky, attic-y look of your standard ad-chocked website"; clutter is another major usability issue which we will be considering.

Most relevant, though, to Senator Grassley's noises about improper commercial relationships was the contrast Heffernan sought to draw between the medical information for headaches as provided by WebMD and the Mayo Clinic website. Googling Mayoclinic.com for "headache Mayo", she reports approvingly that "no specific drugs are mentioned for garden-variety headaches until page 8, when over-the-counter analgesics are mentioned" and she concludes: "It didn't rush me to hysteria, or to drugs." Googling "headache WebMD", however, brought you straight to the heavy stuff, the Migraines and Headaches Health Center, with a picture of "a woman holding her head in agony", scare headlines like *Headaches— when is it an emergency?*—and talk of anti-nausea drugs and medications to prevent and stop headaches.

WebMD mounted a fierce defense (Grossberg, 2011). It insisted that its content "undergoes a rigorous medical-review process to ensure that it is credible and accurate" and that "we always make a clear distinction between our own content and that of our advertisers." (On this, see our own findings below.) It made no direct reference to Heffernan's critique of the presentation of headache information, but instead hit back by impugning the New York Times' motives:

> We would have also expected The Times to disclose its ownership of the advertising-supported health site on About.com, which competes with WebMD.

As of November 2013, the Senate Committee had yet to release any conclusions, but the affair rumbled on for a time. In July 2011 WebMD's share value crashed on reduced profit forecasts due, WebMD said, to extended legal and regulatory reviews which were delaying drug sponsorship from pharmaceutical companies (Associated Press, 2011). In May 2012, WebMD had appeared to take a step closer to Industry, naming a senior executive of a leading drug manufacturer as its CEO (De La Merced, 2012). By July 2013 its share price had bounced back.

Who's in Charge and Who's Responsible?

With Senator Chuck Grassley's words in mind—"many people access WebMD seeing it as an independent, objective medical resource"—we were particularly interested in examining oversight and responsibility at WebMD.com.

Remarkably for a top-ranked health portal, we could find no mention of oversight or responsibility on WebMD's home page. Meanwhile, there appeared to be a prominent content area sponsored by the FDA (right-hand column near the top of the home page). Moreover, another page was presented as a WebMD-FDA partnership. We are concerned that this may convey the impression that the entire site is overseen by the FDA. (There is some evidence that the public thinks all drug ads are FDA-approved.)

> RECOMMENDATION: If portions of a site are under FDA sponsorship or partnership, there should be a prominent statement that the site as a whole is not under FDA oversight.

Authorship of the drug information was also peculiarly hard to determine. Near the foot of the page, in mouse print, we noticed the following:

Information last revised March 2011 Copyright(c) 2011 First DataBank, Inc

But who was First DataBank? There was no link or other indication. And how good was their oversight?

RECOMMENDATION: Oversight and responsibility for medical content should be displayed prominently on the main drug page.

Accreditation—What Does It Really Tell You?

WebMD, and several other big health sites, display accreditation logos. Very reassuring—if you actually notice them. You may have spotted these tiny accreditation logos at the foot of the WebMD home page. But what health-related safeguards do URAC and HONcode actually provide?

Clicking on the URAC logo just brought us to a mystifying form. But googling 'URAC' revealed that "URAC is the largest accrediting body for health care" and that all manner of important bodies have signaled their trust in it—including the Veterans Health Administration. But what precisely are URAC's health website standards? The URAC website stated that you will have to send them a formal request or purchase their handbook (URAC, 2011). This, then, is how the URAC informs the public about the standards that are meant to protect them.

Eventually, we discovered what these standards were. They include a commitment to a clear distinction between advertising and editorial content.

The standards set by HONcode were a lot more transparent. Its *Code of conduct for medical and health Websites*, part 8, stated:

Clearly distinguish advertising from editorial content.

How well WebMD meets these URAC and HONcode standards for separating advertising from editorial content is something we will come to shortly.

RECOMMENDATION: Any accreditation logos should appear at the top of the home page, so that users gain some immediate sense of a site's reliability. The meaning of the accreditation should be briefly indicated right there. There should be indication of date of accreditation and monitoring.

WebMD Content

The Home Page

At WebMD's home page, medical information took up some 60% of the page, and ads just 10%—good for a for-profit health site. The choice of content, as listed for the user in the top menu (> *Drugs and Supplements*), was:

find or review a drug, pill identifier, drug news, mobile drug identifier, find a vitamin or supplement, first aid and emergencies, WebMD community and experts, WebMD ask the pharmacist

Disappointingly, we could see no advice to see your neighborhood pharmacist.

RECOMMENDATION: Drug sites should carry a prominent message "Speak to your pharmacist"

Find a Drug (If You Can)

We visited WebMD drug pages via the WebMD home page and via a Google search. A search for AcipHex Oral promised:

Aciphex Oral : Uses, Side Effects, Interactions, Pictures ...
Find patient medical information for *Aciphex* Oral on WebMD including its uses, side effects and safety, interactions, pictures, warnings and user ratings.

However, approximately 80% of the page was taken up by other content, much of it entirely tangential to AcipHex and full of distracting animated commercials. It made no difference which tab we clicked on. The only AcipHex content was in the central column, in a miniscule font.

RECOMMENDATION: Drug content should predominate at a drug information page.

Promotion or Information?

Recall that WebMD's HONcode and URAC accreditation guarantees that advertising and informational content will be kept distinct—a major quality criterion in health site design.

When we visited, however, the top banner read *Rub osteoarthritis pain away*—and the only indication that this was as an "advertisement" were some letters that we could only read by holding our head at right angles and doing a zoom.

Ads by Google can easily be mistaken for information—take this one for example:

Psoriasis Symptoms
Get a discussion guide for talking to the doctor about your psoriasis
www.psoriasisLiving.com

In actual fact, this web address was a proxy for the corporate drug site http://www.stelarainfo.com/.

RECOMMENDATION: Ads on health websites must be prominently labeled as such.

What of that banner *Rub osteoarthritis pain away*? This was a further evasion of the distinction between promotional and informational content. We landed on a page about Voltaren gel that was a full-page promotion, as the title bar confirmed:

Relieving osteoarthritis joint pain (sponsored)

but that would not necessarily have been clear to the user. To cap it all, the WebMD logo on the page seemed designed to suggest that the page was under WebMD expert editorial control. True, in the middle of the page was a small notice: "The following is a sponsored resource. The sponsor of the content has sole editorial control"—but did this refer to the entire content of the page? Or just what was below these words? It left us uncertain.

RECOMMENDATION: Any sponsorship lines must be prominent at the top of the page and make clear which content is sponsored. No contradictory indication of editorial control should be displayed.

But what actually *is* "sponsored" information? Can one assume that it is impartial, or could it be commercial? Some of the things we saw at WebMD seemed to confirm Virginia Heffernan's trenchant criticisms, referred to earlier. We decided to follow some sponsored links—free of any apparent branding—dealing with conditions, in a section entitled *Health solutions from our sponsors*.

Some of the link names sounded like impartial information, e.g.

Answers about puberty
Reach a healthier weight
Treating depression

By contrast, others, by their tone, were unmistakably promotional, e.g.

Are you depressed?
Nodding on night shift?
Ouch! Treat heartburn

However, even the impartial sounding link names often led to a heavily branded "experience". For example:

Answers about puberty	Unbranded content with a few ads.
Reach a healthier weight	Unbranded content with a few ads.

Treating depression	Strongly branded promotion for Cymbalta.

The heading read "Depression hurts. Cymbalta can help" and in the middle of the page was a small notice: "This content is from our sponsor. The sponsor has sole editorial control"—Did this refer to the entire content of the page? The words would suggest so, though where they were positioned left us uncertain.

Osteoarthritis pain	Strongly branded promotion for Cymbalta.
Chronic lower back pain	Strongly branded promotion for Cymbalta
Bipolar Disorder Facts	Unbranded content, but with full safety information on Seroquel, a Seroquel branded template, and a link to Seroquel—amounting to a subtle branded experience.
Are you depressed?	Strongly branded (identical content to *Treating depression*)
Depression med for you?	Strongly branded promotion for Cymbalta
Inflammatory acne?	Strongly branded promotion for Solodyn

Amid all these heady "branded experiences", we had a hard time reminding ourselves of WebMD's motto: "Better information, better health".

However, there is a peculiar rationale for this practice. In 2009, companies who mentioned a brand name in a link without disclosing the risks right there suddenly began getting FDA citations for violating regulations. They responded with a "solution": using generic-sounding Web addresses that redirect users to the brand's site (Clifford, 2009).

> RECOMMENDATION: As "sponsored" content can run the gamut from pure advertising to pure information, drug sites should make it clear (and be allowed to make it clear) at the link whether a sponsored site is strongly branded or not.

How Well Was WebMD Organized?

In the WebMD drug articles, general presentation was poor. The decision to give just a portion of the screen to the drug article—leaving the greater part to sponsored and templated content—was ill-conceived. Far too much text was packed into a small window and in far too small a font. The effectiveness of "open" formats, with lists and white space, has been demonstrated at websites such as mayoclinic.com.

For instance, the *Side Effects* section tried to present a kind of running text "narrative" but the effect was muddled and dense.

RECOMMENDATION: Whatever the virtues of presenting side effects in "narrative" form, they should be presented as a bulleted list and with clear distinction between urgent and non-urgent cases. Actionable items should be highlighted.

Links were not WebMD's strong point. Thus, the *Interactions* section concluded with a link *Does rabeprazole Oral interact with other medications?*—which led us to a dense, technical list of interactions designed for **physicians**.

RECOMMENDATION: Content for physicians should be labeled as such and kept well clear of content for consumers.

The *Overdose* section was also misleadingly named. It actually dealt with Overdoses, Missed Dosages and Storage.

RECOMMENDATION: Dosage and Storage sections should be clearly flagged.

MEDICINENET.COM (AFFILIATE OF WEBMD)

Medicinenet.com is an affiliate of the WebMD empire. It describes itself (*About Us*) as providing "easy-to-read, in-depth, authoritative medical information for consumers", produced by "more than 70 U.S. board-certified physicians". Medicinenet.com ranked #1273 in popularity for American visitors at Alexa and #355 (estimated) at Quantcast on July 23, 2013.

In 2011, we visited the medicinenet.com main *Medications* page and some of the links there, including the page for Lisinopril: /lisonipril-oral/article.htm.

Who's in Charge and Who's Responsible?

Determining oversight and accreditation of medicinenet.com was difficult. At the home page, we noticed the catchy slogan "We bring doctors' knowledge to you" at the top of the page, but felt entitled to something a bit more solid. Finally, after scrolling (a long scroll) to the bottom, we established that Medicinenet.com is accredited by HON Code. The certificate was up-to-date when we visited ("May 2010—May 2011, last visited 3 Jan 2011").

But should you wish to know about the kind of experts, if any, who have actual responsibility for the site, you would need to ferret a bit further. We could not find a hint of them on the home page. So we went back and googled MedicineNet and then clicked on the sublink *Medications* in the Google result, which brought us to http://www.medicinenet.com/medications/article.htm.

But there was still no hint of where the expert responsibility for the site lay (unless we perchance pursued the miniscule link *About us*). Only when we reached the individual medication pages did we find some answers. Thus, at 'Lisinopril, Zestril, Prinivil' it stated prominently near the top of the page:

Pharmacy Author: Omudhome Ogbru, PharmD
Medical and Pharmacy Editor: Jay W. Marks, MD

Content

Clicking the tab *Medications* at the home page, we arrived at the main *Medications* page. It was largely informational—a wide column headed *Popular medications* ran down the page for six screenfuls, giving 75–100 word descriptions of some 20 medications.

But information for whom? A new visitor might well wonder. The descriptions were all in unbroken blocs of "mouse-text" and in language none too easy to read. Looking about for a clue, we noticed that the title bar read *Medications information—Index of drug monographs produced by pharmacists and medical doctors*. It all suggested that this was information for health professionals. On the other hand, the in-page title sounded consumer-oriented: *Medication A–Z list*. And a little box promised: "Find relevant and reliable information on common medications".

Each medication opened to an article of one to three pages. The content was based on FDA Prescribing Information, and was organized as follows:

generic and brand name (but no guide to pronouncing them)
drug class and mechanism
whether prescription required
form
storage
used for
dosing
interactions
pregnancy
nursing
side effects

In keeping close to the FDA Prescribing Information, the editors did not set out any directives—except for the occasional formal "warning". We looked in vain for directions in an emergency or for a "Call your doctor at once if…" The *Interactions* paragraphs also seemed particularly suited to physicians rather than to the average patient.

In these, and some other respects (see below), Medicinenet.com was not particularly user-friendly.

Alongside the prescribing information, these pages offered other content, such as *Related Conditions and Resources*. Some was quite clearly related to the medication, some less so, and some probably not (e.g. at Lisinopril: *ADHD health check* and *How to raise a kitten.*)

Returning to the main *Medications* page, there was a helpful *Pill Identification Tool*—and on either side of the column of brief descriptions, a cascade of ads and sponsored links, such as *Relieving osteoarthritis joint pain*. It was these sponsored links that caused us concern. Some of them, it immediately transpired, were pushing a brand, e.g. a link *Relieving osteoarthritis joint pain* led us to an ad for Voltaren Gel. Slightly more subtly, a link *Rheumatoid arthritis* led to a slideshow, flanked by a large ad for Simponi.

Where the ads were overt, there were sometimes other questionable practices. One prescription ad bluntly encouraged you to take the drug. Rather than a whispered "Ask your doctor", a condition link *ADHD symptoms: recognize the three key symptom areas* led to a slideshow, flanked by a large ad for Vyvanse—and this ad alternated with an ad for Intuniv that proclaimed "For kids with ADHD 6–17. Download free trial offer."

There was no mention that Intuniv is by prescription only. And in another, third drug ad for Concerta alternating with these two, the only mention that it was by prescription only was in small print, dwarfed by the message "*Get a 30-day free coupon.*"

How Was Medicine.net Organized?

The layout on all these medication pages and conditions pages was cluttered, and more geared to browsing casually than to a directed search. Visually, it wasn't obvious whether the content in the left and right hand columns was related and in what way. The important links to related drugs at WebMD, the box *Report Problems to the FDA*, and the Pill Identifier Tool were overshadowed in the clutter. Even more important, there was no index of contents. And what did appear to be one, a miniscule link *Lisinopril index*, was nothing of the sort—instead, it brought us to a page of 'related topics', some of which were related to Lisinopril, e.g.

> *Medications > ACE inhibitors, high blood pressure medication etc.*
> *Related diseases and conditions > kidney failure, congestive heart failure etc.*

and some quite unrelated:

Doctor's and Expert's Views > Medication disposal, Reducing medical costs.

RECOMMENDATION: Health pages at health portals should be geared to a directed search rather than to browsing casually.

Navigating from page to page was equally muddling. The important sounding section *Suggested Reading on Lisinopril, Zestril, Prinivil by our doctors* was mistitled; it turned out to be a mix of related and quite unrelated articles. Meanwhile, clicking on the *Lisinopril* link brought us to an article *Lisinopril, Zestril, Prinivil* which was relatively well organized. However, when we clicked to continue to page 2 of the article, this turned out to be a *different* article of 5 pages, *Lisinopril—oral, Prinivil, Zestril,* much more detailed but much more dense. We tried to navigate through it, but that wasn't easy: once we reached any of the other five pages, the list of contents vanished and so we could not navigate within the article. Side effects were poorly formatted. The article was marred by dense blocks of text and lack of bullets. Attribution was absent.

We continued to hunt for a list of serious side effects—and eventually our luck changed: Back at the first article, *Lisinopril, Zestril, Prinivil* (p. 1), at an area on the right (*Related Drugs—WebMD Health Network*), we clicked on *Prinivil—RxList,* and halfway down the screen we found a list of serious side effects:

> For patients: What are the possible side effects of Lisinopril (Prinivil, Zestril)? Get emergency medical help if…

But further hurdles lay in store: The rest of that page, and the next 6 pages, were written in professional language—and the tab at the top of the page confirmed that we had been directed unsuspectingly to a section for professionals. Fortunately, there were two other tabs at the top: *Consumer* and *Patient* (what might the difference be between a consumer and a patient?) We clicked on *Patient* and were whisked to p. 11 of the article—and there, at last, we found a user-friendly Q&A and digestible bulleted side effects.

Bad Language

The language of the individual drug articles at medicine.net did not speak to the average user. It was based on FDA Prescribing Information, and unfortunately sounded like it, with plenty of ponderous terms and impersonal style: "Capsules should be administered…, not adequately evaluated…, the physician must weigh the benefits…"

Beyond the obvious difficulties it causes, technical language has symbolic effect. It acts as a "keep out" sign to the majority of Americans. They will quite likely not bother to read beyond the first few seconds.

DRUGS.COM

Drugs.com claims to be

> the most popular, comprehensive and up-to-date source of drug information on-line. Providing free, peer-reviewed, accurate and independent data…
> (home page, July 23, 2013)

It ranked #597 in popularity for American visitors at Alexa on July 23, 2013. We visited the page for Lisinopril: drugs.com/lisinopril.html.

Extra Content

At drugs.com we found all the content (more or less) that you would have found at the government's non-profit PubMed Health site—plus a few extra goodies: pictures of the pill, sign-up for updates, and links to support groups. However, we found no information on how effective a drug is.

But Less Organization

Though accredited by HONcode, the Lisinopril page fell well below the HON-code standards of organizational clarity and division between information and promotion—or the standards of a corresponding Wikipedia page.

(a) Contents List and Site Map

There was no list of contents, and a site map was hard to locate. We had to scroll down many screens-worth to a tiny link at the foot of the page.

>   RECOMMENDATION: Drug sites should provide prominently (a) a list of contents, and (b) a link to a site map

(b) Logical Arrangement of Navigational Links

There were two banner navigation bars linking to general information, one large and one tiresomely small, but there was no logic as to which kind of info was where or why.

>   RECOMMENDATION: Navigational links should be organized logically

(c) Content Cohesion

The major expert content (names of medication, indications, status of medication) was scattered into visually uncohesive blocks. This is hard on many users.

RECOMMENDATION: Major content should be organized logically.

(d) Fencing Between Ads and Information

Despite its obligation under the HON Code accreditation to keep ads and information apart, drugs.com allowed Ads by Google to come between names of medications and their indications, without adequate visual "fencing". Ideally, ads should be at margins so as not to break the information flow.

RECOMMENDATION: Drug sites should strive to position any ads on the margins of information flows.

RECOMMENDATION: Drug sites should ensure adequate visual "fencing" of ads, so that they are not confusable with information content.

RECOMMENDATION: Drug site pages profiling a medication should place all information on the function and use of that drug in an uninterrupted visual flow, segregating other information (e.g. other drugs in the same class) into a separate flow.

(e) Foregrounding Urgent Warnings

The sections "What is Lisinopril?", "What is the most important information I should know about Lisinopril?" and "Side effects" failed to foreground the most urgent elements (e.g. "Do not use", "Stop using the medication", "Get emergency help if…"). Similarly, much more prominence should have been given to the two warnings

a. to tell your doctor about any other meds you're taking
b. not to start any new med without telling your doctor.

RECOMMENDATION: Drug sites should develop standardized methods for foregrounding urgent warnings, e.g. bullets and/or bolding, upper case.

RECOMMENDATION: Drug sites should develop a standard graphics (color-coding?) for distinguishing the three levels of action:

1. Get emergency help
2. Call doctor at once
3. Less serious side effects

RECOMMENDATION: Drug sites should develop a standard prominent line to call one's doctor and/or one's pharmacist for medical advice about side effects, and two standard warnings, to be displayed prominently high up on the home page and on all individual drug pages, (a) to tell your doctor about any other meds you're taking and (b) not to start any new med without telling your doctor.

In the next chapter, we take soundings in the health portals hosted by two long-established names in consumer education and drug dispensing, the Mayo Clinic and the Walgreens chain of pharmacies.

CHAPTER FIVE

Entering a Health Service Portal

MAYOCLINIC.COM

Mayoclinic.com is the site of the Mayo Clinic system of hospitals and clinics, for many years a trusted source of health education. Mayoclinic.com was ranked #330 in popularity for American visitors by Alexa and #106 by Quantcast on July 23, 2013.

The home page of Mayoclinic.com offered entry to an extensive health portal for consumers and health professionals—with no ads or sponsored links anywhere to be seen. The only image was of well-being—a mother and child, older couple and the like—with a large slogan "Answers" and links to *Patient Care* and *Health Information*. The first impression was one of undiluted care and communication.

At *Drugs and Supplements A–Z,* we visited the pages for Lisinopril (oral).

Who's in Charge?

Oversight was prominently marked at the top of the Lisinopril page: "Drug information provided by Micromedex". But there was no link to a Micromedex page, nor any hint as to who or what Micromedex is.

Surprisingly, perhaps, none of the medication articles that we clicked on appeared to carry the name of an individual physician or the Mayo Clinic staff. Presumably, the user will have ample faith in the Mayo Clinic's own "brand name".

Content

The Lisinopril article consisted of five pages, sensibly named:

> *brand names and description*
> *before using*
> *proper use* (which included dosing and missed doses)
> *precautions*
> *side effects.*

Once again, however, we could find no information on how effective a drug is.

Neat Organization

This was a relatively neat and clean experience. The drug information occupied center stage—50% of the width of each page. The rest of the page consisted of Mayo Clinic-related aids, such as e-newsletters, Mayo online community, and a *Health Manager*—and a sponsored link and/or a pictorial ad for a drug. Overall, there was nothing too distracting.

The information itself made good use of subsections, bulleted lists and the like.

How About a "Prompt Box"?

Amid all this neatness, there was a still a need for actionable matter to be highlighted. Curiously, the same deficiencies were showing up again and again.

We would offer a further suggestion to help the low-literate, the elderly, and indeed anyone trying to absorb the gist: A "prompt box" with key actionable words. Thus, a prompt box for the *Precautions* page might read:

> *swelling, stomach pain, fainting, infections, worsening, jaundice*

Such a widget might also make it easier to locate key facts in a hurry.

RECOMMENDATION: Create a "prompt box" with 1–2 word prompts for better absorption and instant reference.

Ads and Information

Turning to the issue of promotion, the Mayo *Advertising and Sponsorship Policy* page stated:

> Mayo Clinic maintains a distinct separation between advertising content and editorial content

It stipulated that advertising content be "clearly labeled as an advertisement" and that "sponsored areas are clearly labeled as such and the sponsoring organizations are identified."

Here, MayoClinic could have done better. The sponsored links and third-party ads were only marked by a tiny *Ad Choices* label. Often, the only identification of the sponsoring organization was in miniscule link labels (e.g. *GinaleSkinCare.com*). Sometimes, the third-party ads ran alongside ads for Mayo Clinic publications—possibly giving the impression that they were Mayo-endorsed.

Language

The vocabulary and syntax was generally clear and simple and addressed the user directly (Flesch-Kincaid grade level: 8.4—allowance must be made for common medical terms), Sometimes, however, it was too stilted—an example:

> The following interactions have been selected on the basis of their potential significance and are not necessarily all-inclusive.

The logical flow and the coherence between sentences was reasonable.

Summary

The mayoclinic.com pages were broadly up to HONCode requirements for their message. We found them relatively uncluttered and well laid out. However, third-party promotion should have been better fenced and labeled. More thought should be given to making key facts easier to find and remember.

WALGREENS.COM

The home page of Walgreens.com provided an extensive health portal, *Health Information,* and an area *Health Shop* with content on various conditions.

Walgreens.com was ranked #294 in popularity for American visitors by Alexa and #176 (estimated) by Quantcast.

Here once again, the quality of prescription drug information was mixed.

Who's in Charge?

There appeared to be two very different systems of oversight. At the A–Z of articles on individual drugs, none of the articles had named authors, and the only attribution we could find was a small line at the foot of the page: Wolters Kluwer Health. No link and no profile for Wolters Kluwer was provided.

Things were much better in the *Health Resources* area: All the articles there—including 20 or 30 *Health Guides* and *In-depth reports*—were authored by named experts and, in addition, reviewed by a body called A.D.A.M, accredited by the highly respected URAC.

Content

There was a lot we liked here. Drug information section commendably offered not only Browse and Search but also *Most commonly referenced drugs* and *Is there a generic equivalent.* Individual drug articles were arranged in well considered fashion:

ingredient name and pronunciation, manufacturer, common uses, before using this medicine, how to use this medicine, cautions, possible side effects, overdoses, additional information.

Equally welcome, drug articles and *Health Resources* articles were ad-free. Even the Walgreens brand name and logo were used discreetly. Typically, the only other content, placed neatly at the margin, was pharmacy resources and drug pricing information.

Organization

In sharp contrast, formatting and arrangement of information at individual drug articles was poor. Many users would probably be unable or undisposed to read them—as literacy experts have long protested, readability is about a lot more than word- and sentence-length. Every section consisted of one unbroken paragraph, sometimes a hideously long one, with no bulleting. The only differentiation was the use of upper-case lettering for urgent information. The *Health Resources* articles, by comparison, were a model of readability.

Language

The language in all the articles we sampled was a pleasure. Technical or ponderous vocabulary was kept to a reasonable minimum. Sentences were short; the authors of the drug articles were clearly under strict orders.

In Sum

Importing information from outside sources has its problems. There is a lot of "swirling content" in the Pharma-sphere, and this is not the first time we have encountered it. What many drug sites need, above all else, is a guiding hand.

CHAPTER SIX

In the Brand's Den

Most common prescription drugs have an "official" manufacturer's brand site, which we refer to as a brand.com site. Much of the drug information that we have explored in the preceding chapters not only connects with the prescription drug itself but also with the manufacturer of the brand. Through this connection, other prescription drug websites acknowledge the brand.com site, refer to the site, or channel Internet traffic to it. And as we showed at the end of chapter 2, many patients prescribed such drugs and seeking to learn more about them online are ending up at a brand.com. For all these reasons, brand.com sites deserve a detailed analysis, background, and critical discussion.

Brand.com sites are doing well, at least for the Pharma industry. As we mentioned in chapter 2, if you were going online for prescription drug information in 2011, there was almost a 50% chance that you were visiting a brand.com site (Rodale, 2011). If manufacturers have been paying the search engine giants such large sums to be placed on the top rungs of their ladder (Seda, 2004), it can only mean that these sites are serving them well. In fact, brand managers adore them: not only are they probably *the* most effective potion for creating "brand awareness" but they also keep the patients coming back for more (Marketing Charts Staff, 2009b).

If we rate prescription drug sites by the number of people who beseeched their doctor for brand x after visiting the brand x website, these were the top ten in 2011 (Manhattan Research, 2011):

> Levitra, Chantix, Cialis, Nexium (purplepill.com), Yaz, Lyrica, Nuvaring, Symbicort, Viagra, Lunesta

Of course, this is not really proof that the websites were responsible. This may actually reveal more about what drugs some patients are eager to try (three of them for erectile dysfunction and two for contraception) than about the effectiveness of a website. A study of statin prescribing has suggested that advertising overall does not increase requests for these drugs—the picture actually varies by type of patient and physician: Ethnicity, education, specialist or primary care (Stremersch, Landsman, & Venkataraman, 2012). Physicians may be pushing back: Prevention Magazine's 2011 survey found that 33% of those asked reported receiving the advertised medication that they talked about with a doctor, a drop from 45%–50% five to ten years earlier (Rodale, 2011).

Across the board, consumer advertising today is focused on building "relationships" between brands and consumers and "engaging" them, to use the marketing buzzwords (Springer, 2009; Argenti & Barnes, 2009). Drug advertising is no exception. A key tactic is to provide medical education and other useful information—and brand.com websites are an ideal platform. The CEO of one ad agency has likened them to inviting guests over for dinner:

> They come to your home, get comfortable, allow you time to converse, serve the food, and then they eat. It's much like the process of coming to a brand site and helping themselves to a meal of interesting content (Boyer, 2011).

The marketers are at work designing eye-catching worksheets and discussion guides, all in the name of encouraging the doctor-patient discussion. Brand managers want to put you in touch with others like yourself, by hosting community discussion boards. They are also scanning these boards for any hint of consumer dissatisfaction. Above all, managers seek to bring you into "dialogue" with the brand itself, which explains the interactive polls and Q&A forums at which consumers reveal their identities to marketers. Any editorial content or other useful information that consumers see at brand.com sites is ultimately designed to bring them back to visit the brand. They may be having some success: Manhattan Research reported in 2012 that 51% of online U.S. adults were using brand-sponsored digital resources, particularly disease management tools, nursing hotlines, financial assistance, and meal plans and recipes (Manhattan Research, 2012). But Manhattan's head of research expected that the brands would need to push further:

Pharma isn't top-of-mind as a destination, so marketers must consider partnering with other health resources such as general health websites, pharmacies and hospitals in an effort to gain traction for these programs (Levy, 2013).

There are thorny ethical issues here of truthfulness and transparency, some of which we will consider here and later in the book. The U.S. Food and Drug Administration is legally bound to protect the public from misleading drug information, as we explain in another chapter. However, when it comes to the rapidly evolving Internet, they have preferred to sidestep these issues. It could be argued that the FDA owes it to the consumer to confront them, and that Congress owes it to America to give the FDA the funding to do so.

As we mentioned in chapter 2, a new ranking policy for prescription drugs was introduced by Google in June 2010. Henceforth, the top result (after any *sponsored* brand.com links) would be a link to drug information from the National Library of Medicine, a non-commercial body. The new feature was developed in a Google partnership with the National Institutes of Health. They license this data from the American Society of Health-System Pharmacists (Ricketts, 2010; Sterling, 2010; McEvoy, 2012) a private sector pioneer in improving medication leaflets. And in November 2012, taking this one step further, Google began displaying a kind of med box: Key facts (side effects, related medications, links to resources etc.) began appearing in the right of the search results page for generic and brand medicines, derived from the FDA, the National Library of Medicine and other government sources—"among others", as Aaron Brown, a Google product manager, put it slightly mysteriously on the Google Search blog *Inside Search*.

THE DIRECT-TO-CONSUMER TV AD—FATHER OF BRAND.COM

How do TV drug commercials compare to brand.com sites? Brand.com sites owe their existence and much of their character to the drug commercials that have been running in American TV networks and magazines since the late 1990s—and on which the Pharma Industry continues to spend heavily. Companies have tended to treat Internet branding as an extension of their broadcast campaigns; regulators too have insisted that Internet branding be regulated as just another form of broadcasting. A comparison between the TV commercials and brand.com sites can prompt some worrying questions for countries in which direct-to-consumer advertising of drugs is still banned from the airwaves but the Internet functions freely.

The American TV drug commercial is a remarkable story of communicative strategizing that has seemed to resolve the incompatible: (a) Seeking to

promote potentially hazardous substances, while (b) meeting statutory requirements—"adequate provision" of sources of information on risks and benefits, and
a "fair balance" to prevent the promotion overshadowing the warnings, and all of
this constrained by (c) the severe space and time limits of the TV slot (usually
30 or 60 seconds on a small screen) and by (d) other cognitive constraints of the
medium: the spoken and written words streaming by and gone (unless you went to
the trouble of replaying them).

Regulators lent a hand, as we mentioned earlier: TV and radio ads were permitted to state just a few major risks, show a 1–800 number, and devote themselves
to singing the praises of the product—as long as these were neither inaccurate
nor obscure. The FDA waived the risk information requirement altogether for
"reminder" ads that simply say "Ask your doctor about x" without mentioning what
x does. Comfortable with the legal protection that a "literal" concept of truthfulness affords (Bolinger, 1980) and unwaveringly committed to the tentative findings of Louis Morris and others on the formatting of TV ads (Morris, Ruffner, &
Klimberg, 1987; Schommer & Glinert, 2005)—where to position the risk information, whether it should be visual or audio, how much of it there should be—the
FDA turned a blind eye to the power of suggestion of the promotional texts and
visuals. In 2008, for its part, spurred by individual "clean-up" initiatives by some
major manufacturers, the pharmaceutical industry issued some voluntary *Guiding
Principles* to address public concern over infringements.

TV drug commercials have come to follow a pattern—combining suggestivity
with literal accuracy and disclosure, using all the tactics that marketers can deploy.
Here are some of the most typical features we have identified (Glinert 2005):

1. Promotion, information and entertainment are blended bewilderingly. A
   voice-over, with no identifiable characters speaking and almost seamlessly
   delivered, uses creative rhetoric to blend promotion and education, i.e. to run
   two speech activities simultaneously. For example: In the context of a string
   of professional summonses ("Continue taking…", "Contact your doctor at
   once"), the promotional call to control one's asthma can take on a professional ring. Touches of postmodernist irony have also become common. Thus,
   one celebrated campaign contrived to mix science with science fiction.
2. Risk messages frequently compete with up-beat music and visuals. Thus, a
   warning caption "Your results may vary" came with an image of a beaming
   woman and a quick-fire string of superlatives. The average viewer may fail
   to grasp that the medication does not always produce a complete cure. The
   less-literate may be particularly challenged.
3. Verbal ambivalence is routine. For example, running through testimonials for an asthma medication, we found a tension between absolute and

relative claims of efficacy. Three of the testimonials were cautious and relative: "gets out *more*", "with *fewer* symptoms", "doesn't have to use his reserve inhaler *as often*", "*more* nights restful sleep", "*fewer* asthma symptoms"—but the fourth testimonial and the epilogue had an absolute ring: "for day *and* for night control of asthma symptoms". Benefits are regularly stated in such a way as to play up their efficacy by implication without making any literally misleading claims. Another campaign seemed to promise cure for erosive oesophagitis ("Relieve the heartburn and heal the damage") while simultaneously conceding: "Only a doctor can tell if you have this damage".

4. The source of authority is often ambivalent. For example, the traditional advertising distinction between personal and impersonal—"company" and "consumer"—is sometimes ostentatiously flouted: characters in the story line can unexpectedly take on the mantle of spokesperson for the product. Traditionally, advertisements employ both an impersonal and a personal footing—a two-pronged credibility strategy. The personal may take the form of characters in a narrative, ostensibly representing the consumer or layperson, and the impersonal a company spokesperson. A powerful instance of the impersonal is the slogan that rounds off many ads.

A brand.com website might be expected to be a very different experience. There are far fewer communicative constraints: It is a place to which one chooses to go—in theory. It does not suffer the same limits of linear time and space that gave rise on TV and radio to the testy "fair balance" and "adequate provision" of risk information; in fact, a website is virtually infinite. However, brand.com is in many ways an extension of the TV commercial—often actually incorporating the TV commercial itself. And in other ways, brand.com has created a whole new set of problems.

"C" FOR CONTENT

Brand.com sites continue to cluster near the top of the search results. What help do they offer? How transparent are they? How well do they meet the legal standards of the U.S. Food and Drug Administration—accuracy, clarity, the full facts, and the risks stated in "clear and conspicuous" form, balancing all the claims to heal. We have pieced together a critical profile of these sites.

As we intimated, companies have tended to treat Internet advertising as little different from a broadcast campaign. They involve the same promotional appeals and even the same images and wording. In principle, though, a website should be far better able to meet the FDA's standards (accuracy, clarity etc.) than a 30 second commercial or two crowded pages in a magazine. It should also be of particular value in the event of a product scare (Kees, Fitzgerald, Kozup, & Scholder, 2008). In fact, a study published in 2005 suggested that a majority of brand sites were indeed providing adequate information as well as a proper balance between benefits and risks (Macias & Lewis, 2005).

But other researchers have been far less sanguine. A sample of 60 brand.com sites, published in 2004, found that just half of them mentioned the drug's risks on the home page (Huh & Cude, 2004). This was clearly mocking the spirit, if not the letter, of the law; to jam the home page with enticing imagery and implicit promises of cure, while burying side effects, contra-indications and so on in a "back" page, where many site visitors will often not see it, could hardly be considered "balance". Indeed, as one Industry observer has noted, risk communication and minimization of risk is the FDA's most frequently cited violation for all media, including the Internet (Murray, 2009).

The FDA has since acted against this aspect of brand.com drug sites: After warning letters were sent out to selected companies, all brand.com sites now post "safety information" on every page.

The same study found further flaws in the way Pharma companies were providing safety information. At 50% of these brand.com sites, the risks were set in smaller font—either an ineptitude in web page design or a deliberate attempt to downplay the risks. Even more inept (for it can hardly be intentional), one quarter of the sites lacked any navigational link to the safety information.

Another sample of 91 brand.com sites, which appeared in 2007, found that only one third of the sites were presenting the drug's risks prominently alongside the health claims (Sheehan, 2007). It was frequently necessary to scroll down to find them—something that many Web users do not happily do. Research has also demonstrated that risk and benefit information are much more quickly found when placed in separate areas at the top of the home page (Vigilante & Wogalter, 2005). This would appear to be sheer common sense, but apparently not for the web designers employed by the Pharma industry. The authors of the study also criticized the multitude of formats on these brand.com sites, which makes it so hard for the user to develop efficient searching habits. (One excellent feature of Wikipedia is the simple, uniform format at every page.) Here again, the FDA was in a position to act many years ago.

Who do health seekers think has actually vetted all this "information", and how recently? Do they even check? Surprisingly little is known about this. A widely-cited study published in 1999 found that many TV viewers thought every drug commercial had been approved by the Government and that only "completely safe" and "very effective" drugs could be advertised (Bell, Kravitz, & Wilkes, 1999). Do people believe the same about all these 'official' drug sites? Disturbingly, those Internet health seekers who claimed to check the sources, disclaimers and the like were found to be doing no such thing, according to a survey published in 2002 in the British Medical Journal. Few even recalled which websites they had used (Eysenbach & Köhler, 2002).

Not that sources of authority are much in evidence at brand.com sites. This issue was already concerning researchers in 2002 (Griffiths, Christensen, & Evans, 2002) and little has improved since then.

THE BIG ISSUES

As we delved further into the jungle of text, image and sound, one set of issues came to concern us more than any other:

- How could these companies promote a brand, while at the same time being helpful and educational?
- Can both these goals be honestly satisfied?

On this depends the Pharma industry's prospects of building trusting relationships with the increasingly sophisticated and "empowered" patient/consumer.

The websites we investigated were the "official" sites of the 100 top-selling prescription drugs of 2007–2009 (Pharmacy Times, 2010) supplemented by observations we had gathered for the years 2001–2006.

WHAT WE EXPLORED AND WHAT WE FOUND

1. Packaging a Brand Site

Meta-linguistic "labels" such as *story, joke, novel, newspaper* help create a frame that sets up expectations and even helps suggest interpretations. Thus, if we know whether we're hearing a joke or a report, we can prepare for whether to believe it—and prepare a suitable response (Tannen, 1979).

a. Is There a Word for a Brand.com Site?

What word do we use for websites of the brand.com type? In popular parlance, brand websites do not appear to be called by any "label" such as "advertisements", "commercials", "articles", "newsletters" or "infomercial". They are simply known as "websites". So we do not give brand.com sites a name that might help us identify them as promotional or informational.

Here are our results for the sites of the 100 top-selling prescription drugs of 2007–2009, examining the link titles and two-line page descriptions in our search results:

The only terms that we could find there were the generic words "site" and "official site".

Even the Pharma industry, always eager to coin a buzz word, does not appear to use any special words for this (Warth, 2000). To leave it vague what a brand.com site actually is probably suits them nicely. So let the user beware: advertising and education are subtly co-mingling, and the meta-language we use does nothing to alert us.

b. Link Titles and Page Descriptions: The Promise and The Reality

We now turn to the websites themselves, or rather, to their "packaging"—the link titles and brief descriptions listed in search results. These descriptions will often influence decisions about whether to enter a site. A title or blurb contributes to the meaning of a text, in much the same way as physical packaging gives products a kind of "meaning". Indeed, they often seem to encapsulate something defining about the work. Thus,

1. With each search result, Google, Yahoo and Bing give a link with a short 'title', created by the site designer. This title also appears as the page header at the home page.
2. Beneath this link is a one or two line "page description" for the home page, automatically generated from the page to be most relevant to the user's query.
3. Beneath that comes the website address (its URL).

But this is what we found: First, compare three drug site descriptions provided by a Google search in 2010. (The three dots are in the text.)

- *Aranesp®*(darbepoetin alfa)
  Manufacturer provides indications, side effects, contraindications and mechanisms of action of this treatment for anemia associated with chronic renal …
- *PLAVIX®* (clopidogrel bisulfate): Help prevent Clot formation for …
  PLAVIX, proven to help protect against future heart attack or stroke. Click for safety and Full Prescribing Information Including Boxed Warning.
- *VALTREX* and Genital Herpes Information—*Valtrebrand.com*
  Genital herpes information from *VALTREX*, the once-daily herpes medication that may be right for you.

The Aranesp description sounded strictly informative, but the descriptions for Plavix and Valtrex contained a mix of information and promotion ("proven to", "once-daily… may be right for you"). There was also a promotional flavor in the Plavix title ("Help prevent…").

We then widened our net to examine the "packaging" of the "official" sites for the 100 top-selling prescription drugs of 2009 as they showed up in our search results. Did they sound informative, promotional, or both?

We searched the 100 top sellers, and found that 92 maintained brand.com websites. Our results for link titles and brief descriptions are as follows:

1. 54% of the sites sounded as if they contained just product information
2. 10% of the sites sounded as if they contained just condition and product information
3. 36% of the sites sounded as if they contained both product information *and* promotion

Thus, only a minority *made it clear from the outset* that they were promotional. Indeed, the majority gave the appearance of being a place to go for straightforward information about the brand.

We should add that, running beneath each page description, there was a URL <brand name>.com. This of course signals that the site is brand-oriented, but one could not deduce from this that the site is promoting the brand.

What we found *inside* the websites was very different. Almost every one of these 92 sites was designed to promote the brand. Taking Valtrex.com as an example: The link provided by the Google search results promised a page of genital herpes information, but clicking on it brought us to a page promoting Valtrex.

This pattern of dissimulation also extended to the page links *inside* the websites. One example: A page at singulair.com entitled *What Exactly Is Asthma?* displayed a prominent *For more information* with a link *to Parent Of An Asthma Sufferer*—but when we followed the link, we found a promotional for Singulair.

The links themselves, however, may be changing. In November 2009, Google unveiled proposals for new "standard" links, to include a fixed warning about major risks (Google, 2009). (See chapter 8 for more details.) Companies themselves are becoming more aware of the risks of a violation letter from the FDA and are sometimes dropping the name of the product from the link description and title—or even removing reference to a disease.

WHAT TO MAKE OF IT

Mixing advertising and consumer education is ubiquitous and in no way peculiar to drug promotion. Advertisers and consumer groups are competing for the same audience and forever maneuvering to outwit the other. In the same way, ad campaigns for non-medical products such as detergents have long cultivated a pseudo-scientific veneer, with men in white coats and pseudo-technical jargon.

As Guy Cook has noted in his discourse-analytical survey of advertising (Cook, 1992), it is the nature of advertising to embed itself parasite-like in other sorts of texts, discreetly feeding on their authority. The savvy consumer seeking drug information direct from manufacturers' sites will need to be aware that advertising is one of the most inventive and savvy fields of human creativity (Cook, 1992).

Even those online health-seekers who have no desire to visit a manufacturer's site may find themselves spirited to one. We tested Google by entering the terms *cholesterol*, *depression*, *hypertension*, and *diabetes*. Top results, in each case, were three sponsored links, but with no visible brand name—and in 9 out of 11 cases they brought us to a brand site, e.g. zetia.com, seroquel.com, victoza.com. This is arguably borderline misrepresentation. Encouragingly, the remainder of the results on the first page, 41 in total, were entirely unbranded and unsponsored (sites like Wikipedia, Mayoclinic, WebMD, Medicinenet). Another non-commercial experience awaited us at migraine.com: Being aware that this website, launched in 2011, belonged to Health Union, a health information company run by two former GlaxoSmithKline directors of marketing, we expected to find ourselves in a heavily "branded" environment—but in fact, the pages we visited were strongly educational. This, however, has not been our experience with all the ostensibly educational sites we have visited.

But how is it, then, that we are not constantly duped by advertising posing as information? Fortunately, the *name* and the *frame* of the text usually betray its intent. When you open a product brochure or watch an infomercial, you rarely need to look beyond the title and the intro. If a brochure baits all the advertising with a little informational content, users will probably know to be on their guard (Martin, Bhimy, & Agee, 2002; Hetsroni & Asya, 2002). The World Wide Web, on the other hand, is still new and rapidly evolving. We lack clear mental frameworks to deal with it; often we do not even possess names for the *kind* of materials we encounter.

2. Ailment, Brand and Other Forms of Confusion

After a landing at a website, the menus are the first place one will generally look to for some orientation—so it is baffling how little thought the designers seem to be giving to organizing these menus.

One might expect menus to maintain a healthy separation between the ailment and the brand. Recall that HONCode has made such a separation a point of honor. But this was usually not what we found. Take the Nexium home page, purplepill.com.

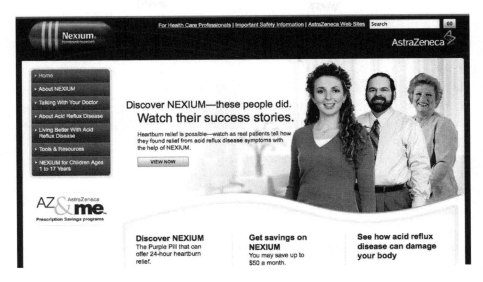

Figure 6.1

Notice the vertical menu on the left. The first and last of the links concern the brand but the middle four concern the ailment. Or consider the row of three links stretching across the page: the rightmost for the ailment but the other two strongly promotional.

Here are our figures:

Of the 100 top-selling drugs sites, just 18 percent kept the condition separate from the brand.

Home pages were particularly heavily branded, which can easily backfire: Information seekers usually skip "in-your-face" advertising using banners, animations and the like (Nielsen, 1999) and obliging them to do so may compromise the credibility of informational content elsewhere on the site.

Many of the sites we visited were just plain muddled—with duplication of content a particular problem. All of this makes it hard to focus on the content and hard to navigate. Web pages that are confusing have been shown to be much less credible (Nielsen, 1997a; Sillence, Briggs, Harris, & Fishwick, 2007). One may wonder why manufacturers and brand agencies have failed to internalize this.

3. Promotional Imagery: The Gorilla on Your Page

The much aped "800 pound gorilla" is a rather apt description of the heavy promotional imagery in commercials for the restricted substances we call prescription drugs. Maybe the most "discordant" visuals (to use the FDA's term for its new bête noire) will be phased out from TV commercials, but now the same visuals have migrated en masse to the Web. In fact, female models bubbling with health decorated most sites in a study of 113 top drugs of 2004 (Naik & Desselle, 2007).

Our own data for the 100 top-selling prescription drugs of 2009 echo this. We did not do a count of health-exuding models, but at 68% of home pages some sort of promotional image took center stage. By "promotional" image we mean images that are suggestive of well-being, quirky, highlighting a free trial, providing a video testimonial, or the like.

At several sites, the promotional gorilla quite dominated the home page. The Safety Information section, meanwhile, was generally tucked discreetly away "beneath the fold". A miniscule "Individual results may vary"—so crucial to understanding a medication—was sometimes almost lost against the large promotional image.

Figure 6.2

There are also other, more subtle forms of promotional imagery. At the abilify.com home page, we found that all the menus for informational content were located within the promotional image and in the same style and color—a clear if subtle attempt to inject brand promotion into help seeking.

Figure 6.3

Even more subtle, and widespread, is the use of a brand design or "livery"—using color, font and images without borders—for the entire home page or even an entire site, as we found at purplepill.com. This may be psychologically comparable to having a brand theme tune running through an ad.

How far this perturbs the regulators in Washington is unclear. Paradoxically, an FDA *Draft Guidance to Industry* in 2009 warned that "problems can arise when parts of a print promotional piece appear so unrelated that the risks do not look to be part of the piece"—e.g. "Risk information is placed in a thin column along the side of an ad in a different font and color scheme" (Food and Drug Administration, 2009b). However, the *Guidance* failed to address what may be a much more frequent phenomenon: information (risks or benefits) *embedded* in promotional hype.

Thus, for most of these companies—though by no means for all—the official website appears to be an extension of their advertising campaign. What then of the legal duty to maintain "fair balance" between the benefit and risk message?

SOMETHING CALLED TRUST

What concerns us is not just the distraction effect but a more fundamental issue of *trust*. If the home page is dominated by promotional imagery, will the user trust it as a source of information? Brand.com sites are not commercials; they do not claim to be such, and they are not referred to as such. If you are visiting them, it is because you have chosen to click to them. And you are almost certainly coming for information.

How users feel or think about brand.com sites is hard to say. Copious research commissioned by the industry is kept hidden away from the public gaze, while little scholarly research has been published—surprisingly, given the public safety implications. We do not know if people identify with the soft-sell imagery so commonly used—such as that inviting trail through the meadow under the slogan *A medicine to help you move forward* at abilify.com. They certainly do not have patience for banner ads, as Jakob Nielsen has shown (Nielsen, 1997b). Do they have a similar impatience with other promotional visuals?

We are also concerned about the popularity of "postmodern" advertising imagery—imagery that plays with and even mocks conventional advertising, using ironies, paradoxes and puns to "throw" the viewer off balance. Do consumers just laugh it off as a joke? Or are jokes of this sort damaging their trust in the informational content?

4. Who Is Really Behind the Message?

What professional authority, if any, lies behind the health information at these brand sites is kept in the background. Often there is no indication whatsoever. Reference to named experts is rare. This too surprised us.

At the sites we visited, the corporation seemed to portray itself as both "end speaker" and responsible party for the entire site. Behind the nameless copywriters and media agencies, what the users are allowed to hear is the company, via its discreet logo and its vociferous brand. Frequently, the brand itself was portrayed as a kind of person, by subtle deployment of human imagery—all part of the grand new strategy of "engaging" with your target audience.

Evidently, the Pharma industry feels so confident in its medical "street cred" that it can dispense with references to identifiable experts or any link to official drug approval information.

Moreover, at 75% of the 100 top-selling sites we examined, the (anonymous) expert advice had to jostle with a product pitch, such as a free offer, a testimonial or a *"how brand x may help"*. Even if the expert advice is objective, it is only one part of the message you are being sent from these brand sites.

5. Accuracy, Hype and Ad-Speak

If a company were to claim that Eczmex (to use a fictitious name) cures 85% of eczema, but could not provide the data to prove it, the regulators would be sending it a warning letter in the next day's mail. For hype and suggestion, however, they appear to have endless tolerance. We have no evidence that people are swayed factually by this kind of thing. However, it does change *attitudes* and *intentions*, which is why companies spend fortunes on it.

Here are just a few of the suggestive appeals in our files:

> *... has been used to treat more than one million people worldwide across all uses*

This Remicade.com message could well suggest effectiveness and happiness more powerfully than that claim that Eczmex cures 85% of eczema—and the cool, smiling male in dark glasses may also be helping.

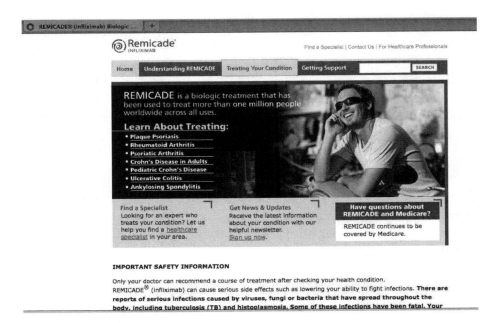

Figure 6.4

Now you can have it all.

Non-drowsy 24-hour relief as well?

Figure 6.5

Angela was born to be wild

And then there's Angela on that Lantus.com home page we showed a moment ago. She may not be suggesting a sure cure but she sure must be socially desirable to some consumers. There is a rather more subtle message at the bottom left of that page: "You may be ready to add or switch to Lantus", hinting that this medication is better and that you just need to wait for the circumstances to be right—and then it will be *your* decision.

IN CONCLUSION

The ethics of drug advertising to the public have been furiously debated, and will continue to be. But despite the apparent gulf between the worlds of medicine and marketing, some observers on both sides have voiced disquiet—and their insightful comments lead us to deeper contemplation:

> Consumers often choose a product on [the basis of] emotional attributes. ... How an emotional appeal fits into fair balance in advertising prescription drugs under the requirements and approval process of FDA is not clear (Liebman, 2001).

Milton Liebman, *Medical Marketing and Media*

The education of patients—or physicians—is too important to be left to the pharmaceutical industry, with its pseudo-educational campaigns designed, first and foremost, to promote drugs (Wolfe, 2002).

Sidney Wolfe, *New England Journal of Medicine*

Prescription drugs are restricted substances, supposedly ringed by regulations to ensure accuracy of information and an adequate and balanced explanation of risks and benefits.

Print and broadcast ads are clearly perceived by the American public as "advertising", and are regulated as such. The Pharma industry intends them as such; it is no coincidence that its advertising excellence awards recognize marketing creativity and sales—but not the education of physicians, pharmacists and patients.

By contrast, brand drug sites have been designed to be both advertising and repositories of technical and consumer information. That is acceptable in principle, and companies and regulators alike have welcomed it: The Internet is an opportunity to provide the kind of product information that the law requires but which cannot possibly be packed into a 30 second TV spot. However, what we have found is a hybrid of advertising and information which existing regulations were not designed to address. It is simply not meeting consumers' needs for adequate and balanced information.

Manufacturers' prescription drug sites have been born in a radically new medium of endless pathways, assembled in a capricious format and an unstable style. The sites themselves are a new, uncertain creature for which we do not even have an agreed name. Internet analysts have also warned that the Web poses severe difficulties for all users, the elderly and less literate in particular.

In the cautionary words of Cary Silvers, Director of Consumer Insights at Rodale, the publishers of Prevention Magazine:

Consumers are more responsive to the 'fair balance' in traditional media due to its familiarity and the recognizable formula. In magazine and TV ads, risk has appeared in a very consistent manner, mainly the black and white page and the voice-over. New and evolving online formats have not delivered the same level of recognition thus far. (Rodale, 2010)

CHAPTER SEVEN

Social Media

THE SOCIAL MEDIA AND YOUR HEALTH

Trust, we suggested in chapter 6, is the philosopher's stone of marketing—and seemingly ever more elusive in the era of the Internet. But Web 2.0, bringing on the user-generated Internet that we call the social media, appears to promise opportunities for a new trust between individuals and groups that have never before been able to connect. And once again, for better or for worse, commerce is finding its way in, and consumers have to be on their guard.

Sixty-seven percent of adult U.S. Internet users were using social networking sites like Facebook or LinkedIn in late 2012, according to a survey by Pew Internet (Brenner, 2013)—83% among ages 18–29, 52% in the 50–64 age range, and 32% among those aged 65+. An Ipsos survey of November 2012 translated this into a remarkable 3.8 hours a day (from a computer or mobile device) for 18–34-year-olds; 3 hours per day for 35–49-year-olds; and 2.4 hours per day for 50–64-year-olds—with women and minorities well ahead of the curve (Marketing Charts Staff, 2013a). Usage in the UK, Germany and Poland was in the same range. As of June 2013, the U.K. Office for National Statistics and Eurostat showed 48% of all UK adults using Facebook and Twitter, surpassed only by the Dutch. Even among British 65 to 74 year olds, almost one in five were on social networks.

And along with friends have come brands. While connecting with family and friends emerged as the #1 purpose in the Pew Internet survey, 35% of online Americans told the Ipsos survey that they regularly check out brand social networking pages—more people than regularly check out those brands' Internet sites (Marketing Charts Staff, 2013b). Here, the Europeans were behind the American curve, at least for the present: the French at 18% the British at 23% and the Germans at 24%.

As for health, almost everyone, it seems, who seeks healthcare online is making some use of social media to do so. These numbers have been sky-rocketing: From 35% of all US adults in 2009 to 60% in the 2010 Prevention Magazine Annual Survey (Manhattan Research, 2009; Rodale, 2010). And of these, 56% said they had used social media to investigate a medical problem, 33% possible treatment options and 32% evaluations of doctors (Carlson, 2011). The long-heralded consumer health revolution of "self-empowerment" is now truly underway.

A commentary on health care and the Internet by the Pew Research Center in January 2010 summed up the role of the social media in this "self-empowerment":

> Social media is simply the current expression of patient activation and engagement. But this time e-patients are part of a larger cultural change that assumes access to information, enables communication among disparate groups, and expects progress. [...] Patients telling each other where to go for treatment, tracking drug side effects for post-marketing surveillance, owning their own data, refuting their doctors' advice, raising money to direct their own experiments ...(Fox, 2010).

The social media may even be the average American consumer's *first* choice for healthcare information. When asked, in a 2010 PricewaterhouseCoopers survey, what kind of source they were *most* likely to use, 56% of consumers said that they were most likely to use media sources and information service companies such as WebMD or iVillage—and just 12% consumer-driven organizations such as Patients Like Me and Angie's List (Anderson & Wasden, 2011). However, Facebook has become the favored home for many communities of patients during the past two-three years.

The communicative essence of the social media is dialogue. The communicative essence of the "traditional" media—if one may assign the term "traditional" to print, broadcast and Web-based media—is monologue.

Some social media are specifically health-related. Patient-community sites are perhaps the best known. Brand-sponsored patient-community sites include

accu-chekdiabeteslink.ca
childrenwithdiabetes.org
crohnsandme.com

Non-brand-sponsored patient-community sites include

patientslikeme.com
connect.diabetes.org
ccfacommunity.org

Other types of social media platform that include health seeking among their extensive uses are video sharing (YouTube), information aggregation (Wikipedia), social networking (Facebook), microblogging (Twitter), user review (Yelp), and social news and bookmarking (Digg Health).

The social media are often described as a globalized version of the old market place: Say what you want—and instantly broadcast it in real time to the World. But the analogy is a simplistic one. What makes the social media so fundamentally different from the old market place is that this is the Internet, with its infinite vistas and its endless opportunity for reproduction and masquerade. As Paul Argenti and Courtney Barnes have noted, consumers are becoming "the ultimate brand evangelists (or brand destroyers)" (Argenti & Barnes, 2009).

Who, then, do consumers feel they can trust to size up a brand? The 2009 Edelman Trust Barometer reported that only two in five Americans and Europeans had trust in the health industry, lower than most other business sectors (Edelman, 2009) and drug manufacturers in particular have been widely condemned over transparency and costs both in the U.S. and in Europe (PMLiVE, 2013).

Added to all these issues are the rapidly evolving platforms and technologies – YouTube, Facebook, smartphones, tablets. The profusion and confusion is perhaps nowhere felt more keenly than in the search for health information.

LIKE ME, LIKE ME NOT: THE PHARMA INDUSTRY, FACEBOOK AND THE SOCIAL WEB

Where anything is being said in the U.S. about a prescription drug for corporate profit, the Food and Drug Administration comes into the picture. Anything about a drug that leads back to the manufacturer, however indirectly, is subject to the laws governing labeling or advertising, which means that it has to be clear, truthful, and balanced in stating risk and benefit.

In July 2010, if you had visited the U.S. website for the leukemia drug Tasigna, you would have been able to click on a button to "share" an image, a webpage description, and a link to the Tasigna webpage on your own Facebook page—all created by the manufacturer, Novartis. But the FDA was not amused. The 100 characters in the page title and the 121 characters of unseen metadata "'fail[ed] to communicate **any** risk information" (Tasigna has a "black box" warning) and omitted some key facts about the purpose of the drug. If Novartis wanted the name Tasigna and its medical purpose to be "shared", it would have to pack its basic risks into those 100 characters, which is not very easy.

In February 2011, YouTube users might have seen a short video that opened with a shot of a physician's office. A sales rep for the osteoporosis drug Atelvia is describing the drug and making claims about its dosing benefits (e.g., "We now have Atelvia that you can eat and drink with in the morning.") The video was posted by the sales rep on orders of a company manager.

The FDA duly issued a Warning Letter: The manufacturers had not submitted the ad for approval and they had failed to disclose risks, indications and full dosing facts (Food and Drug Administration, 2011; Wasserstein, 2011). Why the company ever thought it could get away with this may never be known, but the fact that this was a home-made video may have something to do with it.

The American pharmaceutical industry has been fearful about testing the social media waters, unlike some other business sectors. What is and what is not allowed is too ill-defined, the Social Web is constantly changing, and the FDA itself is uncertain how to impose its authority either on the social media or on the Internet as a whole.

A cold gust swept through the Pharma industry in August 2011, when Facebook withdrew the special privilege that Pharma had hitherto enjoyed of blocking all comments on a page wall. Companies promptly began removing pages for different disorders or patient communities. Thus, AstraZeneca, producer of the antidepressant Seroquel, shut down a page devoted to depression. Pages such as *ADHD Moms* (Johnson & Johnson), *Breakaway from Cancer*, and *Epilepsy Advocate* also vanished. The only kind of Facebook page that companies could henceforth continue to run without a comment wall were prescription product pages (a small part of pharmaceutical company pages).

As the Washington Times saw it, the Pharma industry feared that users "might write about bad side effects, promote off-label use or make inappropriate statements about a product, and that the comments could raise concerns from government regulators" (Torres, 2011).

After holding a long-awaited first public hearing on *Promotion of FDA-Regulated Medical Products Using the Internet and Social Media Tools* in November 2009, the FDA announced that it would not be issuing new regulations or standards for social media. Instead, in December 2011, it issued guidance for responding to unsolicited requests for off-label information—of particular relevance to Facebook, Twitter, forums on WebMD and the like, but nothing approaching comprehensive guidance (Food and Drug Administration, 2012a). Full policy guidance regarding Internet promotion, including social media, is legally due by July 2014.

The Pharma industry has been chafing. But, as a leading analyst told the Wall Street Journal, no one could expect detailed instructions about what is permitted in a tweet or a Facebook comment or sponsored online patient forum—"Media is changing too quickly" (Hobson, 2011).

And so drug companies that wish to speak about their product on the social media must ask their legal departments to make-believe that this is a page of print or a broadcast commercial. Some companies have, indeed, developed a large following on Facebook and Twitter. Johnson & Johnson and Pfizer scored high in the number of Facebook likes, in a study conducted in November 2011 (Cegedim Strategic Data, 2011). Pharma has a strong presence on YouTube, LinkedIn, Flickr and the blogosphere—and not just for an American audience. A combination like Disney and Lilly Diabetes at http://t1everydaymagic.com/ casts a global spell.

Here is where regulatory watchdogs around the globe, waiting to pounce on any drug advertising to consumers, must focus their attention. TV ads made for the U.S. are available on YouTube for all the world to see. So too are brand.com sites. A 2011 study found that some blog sites and Facebook pages "intended for US residents/customers only" were freely accessible to overseas users, while mobile apps were being marketed by Pfizer, Novartis, Roche and others, targeting consumers in Canada, France and Korea (Liang & Mackey, 2011). Interestingly, when we performed a Google search outside the U.S. in 2013 for several U.S. trade name drugs, the search results brought up the brand.com sites but not the Google drug fact box or the website of the National Institutes of Health.

However, direct promotion on Facebook or Twitter—or anything that smells of promotion—is too risky. As Mark Senak put it in his blog *Eye on FDA* in April 2013 (Senak, 2013):

> For some in industry, the lack of guidance has had a chilling effect on participation in social media and even the Internet, despite the fact that it is a resource to which patients regularly turn for information. As a result, digital and social media have become a sort of regulatory bogeyman.

UK regulators issued informal guidance in April 2011 that tweets promoting prescription drugs probably infringe the Code of Practice, and duly issued Bayer UK/Ireland with a first complaint about a Twitter ad for violating fair balance and undermining consumer confidence (Egilman & Druar, 2012).

Drug manufacturers naturally covet the social media. One much trumpeted avenue is for companies to use the social media to "discuss" rather than "advertise" their brands. "Ask your doctor" would be a thing of the past. In the words of one eChannel Marketing manager:

> Many brands want to use these gathering places as a new form of media, to spread brand messages and promotions. But very few brands really understand how to approach the social sphere systematically.

Outside Pharma, spending on ads dressed up as content ("sponsored ads") was set to jump 24% in 2013, with the Federal Trade Commission sighing but saying very little (Launder, 2013). The general public, meanwhile, can say anything they like about medications on the social media—provided it is not said for business purposes. If they wish to upload material related to Lipitor on, say, Facebook or YouTube, there is no legal duty to be accurate, clear or balanced. Of course, it might be unwise for you to post unfounded or promotional information about Lipitor on the social media; you can still get sued for damages. But to do so would not be a breach of the law. The Food and Drug Cosmetic Act was simply never framed with the idea of limiting free speech about food or drugs. It was about protecting the public from misleading commercial speech.

The reality is that the social media are awash with content about prescription drugs that is anything but accurate, clear, and balanced.

YOUTUBE

YouTube Nation

YouTube was launched in May 2005. By 2013, it had a global audience of one billion different viewers watching over 6 billion hours of video each month, a quarter of this on mobile devices. Seventy percent of its traffic was coming from outside the US (YouTube, 2013). YouTube users are not just the young or hip, they are four out of five Internet users (Comscore, 2011). YouTube is now the go-to search engine for many who prefer to hear and see the information they are interested in.

YouTube is a cross between social media and a more "traditional" website (Burgess & Green, 2009; Snickars & Vonderau, 2009; Strangelove, 2010).

1. It is very much a participatory experience: It combines a Google-type search mechanism with lots of 'mom and pop' materials
2. Comments about the videos are prominently displayed
3. The results often trigger a set of response videos

We are all part of two major trends in digital health, according to a Google report in 2010 (Google, 2010):

1. A boom in online health video
2. A scramble for the Mobile Web for our healthcare decisions

Online health videos have been attracting more viewers than even celebrities or cookery. And nearly 50% of consumers reported in Prevention Magazine's national survey for 2009 that online health videos, rather than written text, were their top resource when searching for medical conditions and prescription drug info (Rodale, 2009). In October 2006, Glaxo Smith Kline posted a video about restless leg syndrome. This was effectively a "help-seeking" ad—there was no mention of the company's drug Requip and therefore no legal requirement to warn of any risks. By November 2010, the video had 355,000 hits, and in August 2011 Glaxo Smith Kline launched its own YouTube channel (Egilman & Druar, 2012).

Many other companies have clambered on board with YouTube marketing channels of their own, such as Abbott, Astra-Zeneca, Bayer, Lilly, and Pfizer, sometimes in a variety of languages. And, problematically, some companies have launched YouTube channels that are unbranded or covertly branded.

Where does YouTube fit into the video landscape? It seems that a significant proportion of Americans have been taking their chances with the unregulated pandemonium that is YouTube. The Prevention Magazine 2009 survey found that 9% regarded video sharing sites as a top resource for viewing health videos—trailing 13% who preferred Pharma company sites and 46% who preferred health information sites like WebMD.

Education or Entertainment—or What?

The educational value of video is, of course, incalculable—and it's often fun. When a site hosts video content, we linger on average 25% longer there. If once we had problems following technical info on a video, with today's QuickTime and other streaming technologies it has never been simpler to hit Pause or Review. And the benefits for all those millions of Americans with visual or literacy issues are enormous; what you can't read, you can now often just sit back and watch and listen to.

With YouTube, however, a new factor has entered the equation: With the right camera and software, individuals can post their own video, and the lucky few will go viral. Admittedly, a few doctors have shot to fame with short YouTube TV shows (Jackson, Schneider, & Baum, 2011). But the junk content seems to be growing rapidly and creating a kind of "vulnerable" participatory culture, as Patricia Lange put it in a study of YouTube (Lange, 2010)—and very little is known about how people are using YouTube or what credence they give it.

Viewer Beware

Sorting the wheat from the chaff is difficult, even for insiders. Are there any quality marks or accreditation logos, or any other indicators as to whether something is academic or commercial? Tell-tale domain names perhaps, such as .edu as against .com? We searched in vain. YouTube is the great equalizer;

private individuals, businesses and professional nonprofits can all project the same persona.

Ideally, high-credibility bodies such as the Mayo Clinic or the National Institutes of Health should be creating their own drug information videos and working with YouTube to place them at the top of the search results, just as has been done for Web pages in collaboration with Google.

Of course, some users will actually prefer to listen to a "patient like themselves". But here again, the public has reason to be cautious. As Gaulin (2011) put it,

> Clinicians and their patients need to be aware of misleading information posted by patients or particularly by pharmaceutical companies who often post videos to make it seem like they are coming from a patient when in actuality it is a company advertisement.

Another study, published in 2010, was able to identify 142 YouTube videos with relevant information on H1N1 influenza—of which 61% had useful information about the disease, whereas 23% were misleading (Pandey, Patni, Singh, Sood, & Singh, 2010). Further research is urgently needed (Gaulin, 2011). Our own searches for YouTube videos about prescription drugs yielded results that were, if anything, significantly more disturbing.

The same top-secret mechanism, or "search algorithm", is used in YouTube as in a Google search. (YouTube was acquired by Google in 2006 for $1.65 billion.) We have already referred to the perennial War of Manipulation by which companies try to climb to the top of search engine results pages. The same is true for YouTube results.

However, we could find no disclosure on YouTube's site as to how its *Smart Suggestions* were arrived at. The same was true for the *Related Clips*. (The *Related Clips*, in the right hand column, was the four or five suggested clips that the engine automatically displayed after a clip was watched.)

We have also mentioned Google's system of accepting a hefty fee to place sponsored links at the top of the results. At time of inspection, YouTube did not have sponsored videos per se, but it had something close: *Featured videos*, which YouTube placed at the top of the page for a search by "rating". YouTube explained them as follows:

> Featured Videos will be primarily populated with videos from YouTube's thousands of partners [...] Featured Videos are not advertisements or paid placements, but do feature content from partners with whom we have a commercial relationship.

But what is a "partnership"? According to the YouTube help article *Partner*, it is

> a revenue-sharing program that allows creators and producers of original content to earn money from their popular videos on YouTube [unless they contain sexual,

violent, or otherwise sensitive content]. You can earn revenue from relevant advertisements that run against your video.

This means that YouTube uses InVideo overlay ads, InStream video ads, or AdSense overlay ads, automatically selected to be relevant to the video clip. (We found this all explained in the YouTube help article *How are ads chosen?*) So "Featured videos" are not advertisements but do contain advertisements. A fine distinction.

YouTube users are thus subjected to "advertising ambush" as subtle as the eye-catching links on a Web page that state "Ad" in miniscule lettering.

On the other hand, as we will see, amateur videos are quite capable of ambushing the best-laid advertising campaigns. Indeed, unlike traditional broadcasts, YouTube encourages all manner of immediate responses to materials. It sets up a dialogue of sorts and diminishes the authority of the author of the video material. These responses can take the form of written comments (sometimes hundreds of them, with little restriction on what is said) and occasionally video responses.

Our Drug Searches

What, then, did YouTube have to offer when we performed searches for some popular prescription drugs? Our own comments below on each clip are in italics.

(1) Lisinopril

A YouTube search for *Lisinopril* on February 1, 2011 returned 63 results.

How would users choose between them? In particular, how would they shop for information, as against heavy-duty promotion? We can only guess what they would most likely do; there is little published research.

Very possibly, the average user considers the number of views as much as the title and description. The view counter looks like it could give some clues as to which clips are credible or useful.

However, there is also the title to consider, and here common sense expectations can be stood on their head. Sometimes, as we will show, titles match descriptions. Other times, a cute title has little obvious connection with the product description. In short, YouTube is an unpredictable blend of a trusty old product catalogue and a marketplace where no holds are barred. Caveat emptor.

Lisinopril Ordered by Relevance

Let us take a closer look at the top six results, ordered by *relevance*.

1. Lisinopril

The title and description, and the thumbnail picture of a pharmacist among his shelves, suggested that this was proper information about Lisinopril, and indeed it was: A 'talking head' summary of some of the basic facts about taking the drug, albeit crammed too densely into 1:20.

Caution: You would have needed to do some clicking to establish the credentials of the speaker and of MedicineCoach.com.

2. Healthy Eating : Lisinopril Medicine Side Effects

Again, the content is in line with the title and description. The speaker identifies herself as Christine Marquette (spelling? Her name is not captioned), a registered licensed dietician.

3. Lisinopril

An unidentified lay-looking middle-aged woman, dressed casual working class, delivers a general description, ending "Talk to your physician about Lisinopril. Lisinopril, in conjunction with exercise, and a proper diet, can help attribute [sic] you to a healthy lifestyle." She sounded like she was reading a script from an expert short description, but the word "attribute" was so inappropriate that we wondered about this.

This is a striking example of the credibility issues of so many of the results we got for prescription drugs on YouTube.

One particularly challenging policy question: Could down-home, amateur presentations be more effective, for some people or for anyone, than a slick professional job?

4. CCSVI and Lisinopril

The title and brief description sounded like they might be expert knowledge but, rather as in #3, this turned out to be an unidentified lay-looking middle-aged man, dressed casual working class and with an unmade bed in the background. He was clearly speaking off-the-cuff—and as a layperson.

5. Lisinopril and Mini-Gastric Bypass

A real-live expert commentary by a surgeon, just prior to surgery, to his trainees. The title made it amply clear what the clip was about.

6. Lisinopril Commercial

The title "Lisinopril commercial" was quite misleading; this was not a commercial in the normal sense of the word but a student's pharmacology assignment.

The number of views was revealing: The health series #1 and #2 had a much higher number of views. It may also be relatively easy to distinguish a home production from a corporate production, as it was here. If there is no description, caution is called for. The thumbnail graphic sometimes helps. #5 had a picture of a surgeon in an operating theater.

Related Clips

We mentioned that the YouTube search algorithm automatically, and mysteriously, displays four or five suggested clips (*Related Clips*) after you have watched a clip.

After watching clip#2, the algorithm suggested these five. Three of the five (2, 3, 4) lacked all medical credibility.

(1) Are You Tired of Your Blood Pressure Medicine?

http://www.iHealthTube.com
[Expanded description]
Robert Kowalski on why many blood pressure patients stop taking their prescription medications. He says some feel the risks of heart disease outweigh the side effects of prescription drugs. More on www.ihealthtube.com

(2) Lisinopril—Here's Something Better!

http://www.youtube.com/watch?v=SPx9HicacyU&NR=1
[No description given]
This is a wacky NON-medical clip

(3) lisinopril—DON'T DO IT, this is Better

http://www.youtube.com/watch?v=iJJlZIFhGQ4&NR=1
[No description given]
Another wacky NON-medical clip

(4) Lisinopril

http://www.youtube.com/watch?v=xmQ_Hj2AMyk&NR=1

[No description given]
Identical with #3 in the preceding list. See our comments there.

(5) Healthy Eating : How to Increase Your Metabolism Naturally

http://www.youtube.com/watch?v=YgOLHhkwX_w&NR=1
[Expanded description]
There are a number of things a person can do to increase metabolism naturally, including physical activity with exercises that alternate between cardiovascular and strength training. Learn about foods with thermogenic properties, such as green tea, with help from a registered and licensed dietitian in this free video on exercise and metabolism.

Lisinopril Ordered by Rating

Ordered by *rating*, on the other hand, the top five results (i.e. our first screenful) were as follows. #1 was a "featured video", provided by a "partner" (see explanation above):

1. Healthy Eating: Lisinopril Medicine Side Effects

Lisinopril is a blood pressure medication that can cause a few side effects, such as hypotension, coughing, adema and facial swelling. Learn about …
by ehowhealth | 1 year ago | 4,350 views

> *Identical with #2 in the list by relevance above. See our comments there.*
> *followed by:*

2. Sexual Healing—Sexual Dysfunction and Impotence

… Sexual Dysfunction sexual dysfunction disorder female treatment **lisinopril** ssri in women citalopram antidepressants and association clinic woman …
by askashaman | 6 months ago | 46 views

> *The title sounded off-topic, and the incoherent description suggested that any connection with Lisinopril was sheer manipulation. The video confirmed our suspicions.*

3. Random video-Hypoglycemic Scare..Ugh!

Comment and subscribe! 0swissmiss0.blogspot.com … "weight loss" diet diabetes hypoglycemic obese skinny girl fat healthy metformin **lisinopril** …
by 0SwissMiss0 | 2 months ago | 35 views

> *Like #2, the title and description made it clear that any connection to Lisinopril was tangential.*

4. SoGood.TV: Healthy Choices and Easy Vegetable Side Dishes

sogood.tv Heather Johnston discusses Food Matters, Mark Bittman's new book on "eating that is healthy for your body and the planet," reports on ...
by gordoneriksen | 1 year ago | 5,461 views

> *Again, as the title and description indicated, this had nothing to do with Lisinopril. How did find its way into our results?*

5. Ace Inhibitors Discover the Benefits and the Risks Associat [sic]

that many people take this particular type of medication i ... ace inhibitors angiotensin receptor blockers beta calcium channel diuretics **lisinopril** ...
by aceinhibitors1 | 3 months ago | 316 views

> *When we actually clicked on #5, we found no attribution on the video or at the page. The page description stated:*

http://ace-inhibitors.com/
Ace inhibitors are widely used to treat a number of different medical conditions, but there are both benefits and risks associated with the medication. The common reason that many people take this particular type of medication...

> *And when we followed the link there, http://ace-inhibitors.com/, it took us to a site that gave no immediate clue as to the source and whether it was sponsored or promotional. Lewis Carroll might have called this a 'White Rabbit experience'.*

Again, our results were very mixed. Only two out of five seemed to be relevant: The title and brief description suggested that #1 and #5 were an informational health series of some sort. #2, #3 and #4 seemed completely irrelevant to Lisinopril.

(2) Searching Zoloft and Plavix

We conducted similar YouTube searches for Zoloft and Plavix. Space only permits a few "highlights".

Brand Promotion? Unbranded Sponsorship?

1. How to Treat Anxiety Disorders with Zoloft

by livestrong | 6,934 views

The full description of this video clip was as follows:

Zoloft is frequently prescribed to patients by their psychologist, and usually takes two weeks to take effect. Learn how to treat anxiety with Zoloft from a licensed professional psychotherapist in this video.

> *This description already raises a possible issue:*
> *It has the ring of a drug commercial ("Learn how to treat x with y"). However, it presumably does not need to meet the FDA's rules requiring "fair balance" between benefits and risks, because it is not commercially sponsored. **Or is it?***

> *The speaker herself is identified as Dr Carol Arvon, a licensed clinical psychotherapist. This being a public message, we would expect something along the lines of "If your doctor has prescribed Zoloft,…" However, at 1:43 on this clip, this licensed practitioner says something extraordinary:*

> *"So the five important things to remember about anxiety are:*
> *Go to your doctor to get your medication with Zoloft". (etc etc)*

> *— Is it professionally correct for a practitioner broadcasting to the public to advise use of a particular prescription drug?*
> *— Does this fall under FDA jurisdiction, or is this quite simply not a commercially sponsored promotion?*
> *— Are there any commercial ties that the practitioner should be disclosing?*

2. Zoloft Commercial

it's a bloody prescription drug, what a [sic] irresponsible TV ad
by lemsipGY | 4 years ago | 187,380 views

> *This one appears to have gone viral.*
> *It was labeled as a commercial, which indeed it was. One would hope that the same is true of all prescription drug commercials. **But is it?***

> *However, this clip beautifully illustrates how carnivalesque YouTube can be and how crucial the framing and context of a clip are to its meaning and impact. The actual video was, as the title indicated, a genuine Zoloft commercial. However, it was framed by a short "description" added by whoever uploaded this commercial: "it's a bloody prescription drug, what an irresponsible TV ad"—quite possibly giving a coup de grace to the commercial.*

This was not where the "carnival" ended. On our visit to this so-called "Zoloft commercial", we found three video "responses" by other users. One was overtly resistant to the commercial message, the second subtly subversive, and the third a veritable parody of subversion:

(a) Zoloft Recall (fig. 7.1) was an attack on Zoloft, with the following description:

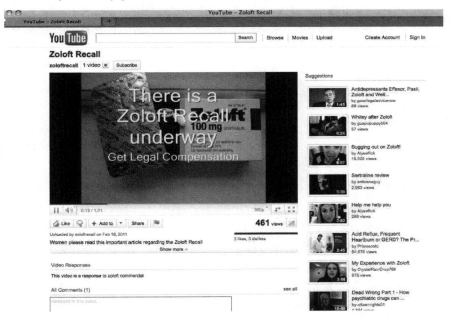

Figure 7.1

Women please read this important article regarding the Zoloft Recall http://www.articlesbase.com/womens-health-articles/zoloft-recall-lawsuit-wome... Claim legal compensation if you've been affected by Zoloft, we need to stand up against the manufacturers of Zoloft and be heard

(b) Depression was a parody of a depression drug ad: A tongue in cheek description of depression, ending with a plug for a spoof drug Limit (limoectopine comedicus)

(c) Canibliss, "the last prescription you will ever need", was a postmodern parody of a depression drug ad, with the goofy allusion to cannabis and the suicidal Golden Gate providing a parody of a parody.

3. Zoloft (Sertraline Hydrochloride)

A pharmacist explains how **Zoloft** works, why doctors prescribe this antidepressant, and common side effects of the drug. Watch More Health Videos at ...
by illumistream | 3 years ago | 54,069 views

> *Here, at last, YouTube came into its own as an effective vehicle for delivering clear, accurate and trustworthy information. The medical authority of the clip was clearly given in an opening caption: Sandra Takami, PharmD. Memorial Sloan Kettering.*

> *This clip was provided by a health video provider, Healthguru.com, which supplies videos (957 listed on June 2, 2011) for the YouTube channel Illumistream*

4. Plavix Suspension

plavix meds free at Walgreens can you take aspirin with **plavix** basilar occlusive disease **plavix** aspirin warfarin **plavix** visual **side effects** tooth ...
by 247e3028 | 2 years ago | 433 views

> *We hope the FDA (and Walgreens) are onto this kind of thing. This is an ad for an online pharmacy that sells Plavix without a prescription. It makes no mention of side effects, despite the search term "side effects", nor is it related to Walgreens Pharmacy, despite the mention of Walgreens in the description.*

> *A possible pointer to this kind of ad is the disjointed description, which may be the result of attempts at so-called "black hat" manipulation of the search algorithm.*

Summing Up

Our YouTube trawl landed a slippery mix, ranging from the informative through the promotional to the satirical and the downright off-target. A growing number of consumers is scanning YouTube results for the right clip. However,

- only **16 of 47 results (34%)** for the three drugs we investigated gave a first impression of *trustworthiness* and *relevance*—and in not one case did this come across as a certainty, let alone a medically authoritative one.

And the results bore this out:

- in **22 of 47 results (47%)**, the clip had nothing to do with our search term. Moreover,
- in **10 of 47 (21%)** the titles or brief descriptions were misleading.

Thus, we found YouTube to be neither a user-friendly nor a transparent or credible source of prescription drug information.

If brand managers are serious about resonating with "activated" patients seeking information and support, and about sounding themes of hope and self-empowerment (to quote the founder of an online patient forum), little of what we saw on YouTube will contribute to these noble goals.

Legal Footnote

Many YouTube users may be getting some of their prescription drug information by an altogether different kind of search. Searches for unbranded information such as allergy are yielding branded clips such as commercials or informational clips about specific allergy brands. YouTube is thus following a familiar pattern found in Google searches: a non-brand website re-directs you to a brand site.

It has been suggested that there may be grounds for legal action if a product name appears in a URL (or in the case in hand, in a YouTube title) or brief description without any mention of risk information or direct link to such, as noted earlier in this chapter.

YouTube health information seekers outside the USA may also be watching American drug commercials there. We were able to watch several 2013 commercials for top-selling drugs and many more going back at least ten years from locations outside of the United States.

WWW.PATIENTSLIKEME.COM

A Website with a Noble Mission

If YouTube encompasses some of the best and the worst that online video-clip sharing can offer, PatientsLikeMe is a harbinger of the good things the social media can achieve for medicine and health.

PatientsLikeMe allows members to share personal details about their conditions and treatments with the membership—and to view a broad profile of the condition and treatment, based on what other members have reported. As of November 2013, it had over 220,000 patients spanning more than 2,000 conditions.

Membership is limited, broadly speaking, to diagnosed patients, caregivers, health care professionals, and guests with "legitimate, non-commercial" interests. (*Membership Eligibility* page)

The website set out two clear and quite distinct goals at its *FAQ* and *About Us* pages:

1. To accelerate research by synthesizing previously unavailable grass-roots data to physicians, researchers, pharmaceutical and medical device companies. For example, the PatientsLikeMe Drug Safety Manager "will review information throughout the site (i.e., profiles, forum discussions, surveys, treatment reports, etc.) to find drug safety information that may be a side effect, and reportable to manufacturers and/or the FDA."
2. To inform patients and caregivers of what is working for others, thus providing them with the information they need to make important treatment decisions with their doctors.

The first of these goals envisions long-term benefits for the entire health system; the second promises the immediate benefit of obtaining and sharing health information.

The broad mission that PatientsLikeMe claims for itself as "Our Philosophy" is a sweeping one: To enable the patient to "effect a sea change in the healthcare system".

How It Works

Members are invited to provide both open-ended and structured feedback about the medications they have been using. Among the structured feedback channels are the Side Effect Survey and the Treatment Evaluation Report, which includes effectiveness, the burden of taking the drug, the cost, and general advice and tips to share with other members.

Non-members can also view some elements of the site. Thus, 3394 were taking Gabapentin, of whom 617 had "decided to publicly share their profiles" to non-members; and 713 were taking Lisinopril, of whom 166 had decided to publicly share their profiles to non-members. Similarly, the site hosts member-only forums and enables one-to-one interaction.

We inspected the site as guests in July 2011 and also conducted interviews with company managers. We had two broad questions in mind:

1. Arriving on the PatientsLikeMe home page, what impression does the user get of the purpose of the site?
2. What type of drug information does the site actually provide to the public, and how good is it?

We were not concerned with symptom information, which may be an even more important element in the mission of PatientsLikeMe.

Looking up a Specific Drug

When we looked for information on specific drugs, PatientsLikeMe offered the following features:

1. Browsing or search by treatment, symptom, and condition
2. Each *patient* had a code name and *profile*, offering:
   self-description ("about me")
   weight history
   condition history (e.g. hospitalization, relapses, symptoms)
   treatment history
   "quality of life" history
3. Each *treatment* had a link to a *Treatment Report*

The *Treatment Report* offered (1) an overall profile of the treatment and (2) individual patient self-evaluations—for the following:

> reported purpose and efficacy
> reported side effects
> reported dosages
> reported stop reason
> reported duration
> reported adherence, burden and cost

There was a further link to "more information, including instructions, precautions, side effects, and interactions". Members could also link to a forum discussing the drug.

We were told that PatientsLikeMe tries to retain the patient's personal health vocabulary—their "user voice"—while coding the comments for the company's database, to be turned into the colored charts that the patient sees. However, as the company told us, the end-terminology is far from clear to patients, who have their own very different ways of talking about things like "pain"; much thought was being given to ways of improving this.

Patients also had the option of adding *Latest Side Effects* and *Advice Tips*. There was a box for users to award marks for helpfulness.

Impressions of PatientsLikeMe

PatientsLikeMe presents itself as a trustworthy medical platform. Members may input personal medical information in confidentiality and obtain certain kinds of medical information that have been designed to be useful and monitored for reliability.

Presumably, members and guests will be aware that the value of the member-provided medical information at PatientsLikeMe is only as good as the completeness and accuracy with which members profile themselves and report on their treatment. Users will also presumably expect that other users' comments have been screened for any misleading information—although there is a disclaimer about screening in the User Agreement.

We were told that patient forums are moderated with a light touch. Patients' beliefs are important grist to understanding their experiences.

What value PatientsLikeMe members attach to the site was the subject of a peer-reviewed study by the site's creators (Wicks et al., 2010). A total of 1323 participants responded. Aficionados of the site may well have been more keen to respond, so the figures should be treated with a little caution. Regarding medications, 57% of users said they found the site helpful for understanding the side effects of their treatments, 37% found the site helpful with decisions to start a medication, 27% to change a medication, 25% to change a dosage and 22% to stop a medication.

Some of the Patient Evaluations featured a paragraph entitled *Advice/Tips*, and this also appeared in the thumb-nail evaluations at the *Treatment Report* page. But is this appropriate? Using the word "advice" or "tip" as a heading suggests that the site endorses this as legitimate advice, which of course it does not.

Ad-free Zone

How far are PatientsLikeMe members shielded from commercial interests? They will no doubt welcome the stipulation in the user agreement that members must be patients, caregivers or health care professionals. They may also have noted the requirement that "Members of PatientsLikeMe with individual commercial interests may not solicit or overtly promote their products or services within the Member Area".

More striking, perhaps, to the ordinary user is that there are no ads—at least, not at the time we visited the site. The FAQ page spelled this out as current company policy, and explained this remarkable fact by mentioning that PatientsLikeMe shares its members' data with industry (PatientsLikeMe, 2013):

No, we're not pursuing an ad-based business model right now. We want to preserve the sanctity of your experience on the site. Our business is based on aligning your interests as patients with industry interests. To do this, we share your data and experiences with industry to help them better understand the real world course of diseases.

The site seemed to live up to its claims of a no-ad policy. It was also revealing to see how uncluttered the page was when there were no ads or other incentives. It was actually rich in white space, so different from the chaos of a typical health portal. All that there was in the right column was a small set of links to individual patient profiles, a link to *All Symptoms*, and a link to a member forum for *depressed mood*.

Reference Guide or Patient Profile?

How far (disclaimers aside) does the site PatientsLikeMe come across as a reference guide—as against a profile of what some patients are reporting about their own experiences? We could not find any wording on the home page that made it clear what PatientsLikeMe offered.

In a sense, PatientsLikeMe is indeed a kind of reference guide. The sheer quantity of aggregated data derived from individual patient reports and presented as user-friendly colored pie charts and bar charts provides patients, physicians and other users with solid data on usage and effectiveness, of a kind not commonly available to patients elsewhere on the Internet.

True, some such data could be misleading. Thus, a patient who learns that the side effect s/he has been experiencing is one of the commonest may be erroneously tempted to dismiss it as insignificant. For example, "weight gain" comes out as top side effect for pregabalin, and yet the *What is pregabalin?* page listed "rapid weight gain" as a serious side effect requiring a doctor to be immediately notified.

A more remarkable feature of the members' data at PatientsLikeMe was the high reported use of some drugs for purposes *not* approved by the FDA. A study of PatientsLikeMe published in 2011 found that "less than 1% of nearly 2000 patients taking Modafinil and 9% of nearly 1400 patients taking Amitriptyline reported taking each drug for purposes approved by the FDA" and added that "We were surprised to find that in two relatively well-understood drugs, the vast majority of uses were off-label" (Frost, Okun, Vaughan, Heywood, & Wicks, 2011). This could raise eyebrows with the drug regulators. However, it is PatientsLikeMe policy not to signal to the patient that a use is "off-label".

Although PatientsLikeMe is not your conventional reference site, the company told us that patients do want to know: "How do I compare with what is conventionally known about this drug?" And so the company were busy thinking about how better to incorporate conventional knowledge into the site, as "context" for the patient-generated information that makes PatientsLikeMe so special.

WIKIPEDIA

What Really Is Wikipedia?

It is hard to believe but Wikipedia was only launched in 2001. Wikipedia is one of the largest and most successful reference sites on the Web, used by 59% of American Internet users as of early 2012 (Pew Research Center, 2012).

Wikipedia is a "wiki", meaning that anyone and everyone may contribute, in principle (Wagner & Majchrzak, 2006–7). Articles are not written by some invited set of experts. This sense of a vast chorus of voices is one of our reasons for classing Wikipedia with social media sites, such as YouTube and Patients-LikeMe—although it is a very special kind of social medium, as we explain below.

In practice, Wikipedia is written largely by a small army of volunteers, many of them amateurs but some with the expert knowledge to produce high quality articles (Arazy, Nov, Patterson, & Yeo, 2011).

At the same time, Wikipedia is governed by a plethora of policies (governing such matters as layout and point of view), crafted by its founders and its semi-formal inner circles. There is no formal hierarchy but consensus. The whole thing is not unlike a family, or even better, an organism, constantly ingesting and evolving.

Wikipedia embodies the massive shift in access to expert information ushered in by the World Wide Web. Web browsers and search engines retrieve information previously seen only by scholars and librarians, except that we usually ingest the information raw rather than intelligently processing it into "knowledge".

To justify this "any author" policy, Wikipedia demands "neutrality" of viewpoint and transparent, reliable sources ("verifiability"). At the same time, Wikipedia concedes that many entries may offer misleading content:

> Older articles tend to grow more comprehensive and balanced; newer articles may contain misinformation, unencyclopedic content, or vandalism. Awareness of this aids obtaining valid information and avoiding recently added misinformation (Wikipedia, 2011a).

But can such a system produce credible information? This is a question to which we now turn.

How Credible Is a Wikipedia Entry?

In General

Policies are one thing, practices another. And with an operation launched on such a massive scale—and into such uncharted waters—policies and practices are bound to drift apart.

Anonymity

Nowhere in an article may one find the author's name. The policy of anonymity makes it impossible for users (and, astonishingly, even editors) to evaluate authors' credentials or investigate possible conflicts of interest. The only thing that authors must divulge is their IP address or username and their editing history, which will mean little to most Wikipedia users.

For commercial interests, such as the pharmaceutical industry, the potential for manipulation and mischief is immense.

Neutrality

The "neutrality" policy prohibits the anonymous authors from expressing opinions or advocating public action. Ironically, however, professional journals themselves frequently advocate public action, issuing warnings or demanding change. But when we come to look at Wikipedia entries for drugs, we will see that warnings and directives are conspicuously absent.

Verifiability

Wikipedia's much trumpeted "verifiability" is really nothing of the sort. It speaks of providing transparent, reliable sources, but this is only as good as these sources really are. For example, there is a wide difference between prestige peer-reviewed journals and what appears in our newspapers. To assume that published material is factual and in-clusive, in the words of Santana and Wood, "is simply naïve" (Santana & Wood, 2009).

The overall "look and feel" of a Wikipedia page may lull you into a sense of mis-placed trust. In particular, the academic footnotes can easily give an impression that the authors themselves are experts, rather than the enthusiastic amateurs that many are.

Wikipedia's reassurances that their editors are hard at work weeding out omissions and falsehoods must be judged by the record. A 2007 study cited in *Wikipedia:Reliability of Wikipedia* stated that "42% of damage is repaired almost immediately... Nonetheless, there are still hundreds of millions of damaged views" (Priedhorsky, Chen, Lam, Panciera, Terveen, & Riedl, 2007).

At the same time, in the scientific realm Wikipedia attracts abundant expert input. (Maybe this is a scientist's equivalent of the afterlife.) A test of science content at Wikipedia and *Encyclopedia Britannica* found an average of just 4 inaccuracies per entry in Wikipedia versus 3 per entry in the *Encyclopedia Britannica* (Giles, 2005).

For Medications

Possibly the first evaluation of medication-related Wikipedia, published in *Annals of Pharmacotherapy* in 2008, assessed 80 Wikipedia entries for common and potentially dangerous drugs (Clauson, Polen, Boulos, & Dzenowagis, 2008). Factual errors were few and far between, but there were major gaps: side effects, contraindications, and drug interactions were sometimes missing entirely—precisely the kind of health-threatening omission that we will demonstrate in our own inspection. Wikipedia compared poorly with the expert-authored Medscape Drug Reference.

Another unflattering study (Lavsa, Corman, Culley, & Pummer, 2011) has inspected the Wikipedia entry for each of America's 20 most frequently prescribed drugs. Out of the 20 elements of information typically provided in package inserts, it found on average just twelve. Moreover, seven of the 20 entries cited no references. Wikipedia's entries for the most common inpatient procedures have also been adjudged to be accurate but frequently incomplete (Devgan, Powe, Blakey, & Makary, 2007).

On the other hand, comparison of the English Wikipedia and the website of the US National Cancer Institute for completeness and accuracy of osteosarcoma-related information found that the English Wikipedia entry was good (Leithner, Maurer-Ertl, Glehr, Friesenbichler, Leithner, & Windhager, 2010).

Gaps and Fingerprints

A pattern appears to be emerging of Wikipedia articles that are accurate as far as they go but not particularly complete.

If this is the case, there is a plausible explanation: Wikipedians, devoted amateurs that they are, are far better equipped to see the small picture than the broad one—rooting out small errors of fact like some army of rodents, rather than sensing broad gaps, the forte of specialists and theorists. This is hardly the "wisdom of the crowd" or the "collective intelligence" for which Wikipedia has been so rousingly celebrated in some circles.

Damaging revelations about the fingerprints of big business on Wikipedia have also surfaced from time to time. A New York Times feature in 2007 reported that hidden hands at PepsiCo and at Diebold had deleted paragraphs critical of those corporations, and that someone inside Walmart had tinkered with an entry about employee pay (Hafner, 2007).

Pharma companies have not been innocent: In that same year, according to the London Times, someone on a computer registered to Astra Zeneca went and deleted claims that Seroquel made teenagers "more likely to think about harming or killing themselves"—while an advocacy group asserted that a computer at Abbott Laboratories had been used to delete references to a Mayo Clinic study about the risks of Abbott's arthritis drug Humira, as well as negative articles about Abbott's weight-loss drug Meridia (Rost, 2007; Goldstein, 2007).

However, Wikipedia has not remained indifferent. It has tried to stay one step ahead of attackers by developing ever smarter software. A tool called WikiScanner has proven able to trace edits back to the computers from which they were done. Unsourced edits trigger the attention of Wikipedia's robots, and recent edits may land on the desk of the volunteers of the Recent Changes Patrol (Wikipedia, 2011b). Nonetheless, the warnings posted at *Wikipedia:About* should be taken seriously: "Newer articles may contain misinformation, unencyclopedic content, or vandalism."

Wikipedia and Brands

Searching for brand name drugs on Wikipedia, we had to look up the generic. Wikipedia policy appeared to prohibit articles for prescription brands—though we could find no overt statement to this effect. When we searched for Wikipedia articles on the 20 best-selling US prescription drugs of 2010, we only found articles for the generic. And, as we noted earlier, these articles showed up on the first page of Google results every time.

By contrast, over-the-counter pharma brands, insofar as we found them, were given some very mixed coverage—without the kind of content control that we associate with the Food and Drug Administration:

> *Tylenol*, consisting in large part of a *Dangers* section;
> *Advil*, consisting mostly of *History*, also *Advertising*;
> *Sudafed*, consisting of *Active Ingredients, Regulation on Sale*, and the history of alternatives;
> *Benadryl*, a brief entry with history, generic and scientific names, use and mechanism

How People Actually Use and Perceive Wikipedia

How people use Wikipedia and why, and what they make of it, has barely been investigated. Ironically, these are precisely the issues that are so important in evaluating what Wikipedia has to say about prescription drugs.

A major reason for Wikipedia's popularity is the high position it enjoys in the search engine stakes. In a search for medical information, Wikipedia health articles appeared among the top ten Google non-sponsored results in 70% of cases, outranking any other health information site, according to a study published in 2009 (Laurent & Vickers, 2009). Wikipedia also provided articles on a wide range of conditions, including rare diseases, again outshining MedlinePlus and other portals.

It also helps that Web searchers seldom look beyond the first page of results (Morahan-Martin, 2004). And there is the familiarity factor: Pages are all laid out to a simple, uniform plan. With Wikipedia, you know what you'll get.

This all translates into viewing. Wikipedia articles are being viewed as much as MedlinePlus Encyclopedia pages. Even in a national health crisis, Wikipedia has been a place to turn. During the swine flu scare of 2009, Wikipedia's entry *Swine influenza* attracted 1.3 million hits on two successive days (Wikipedia, 2011c). Medical students are no exception: An Australian study of computer study sessions by 842 first to third year medical students found that Google and Wikipedia were consulted far more than eMedicine or the National Institutes of Health site (Judd & Kennedy, 2011).

But what do people actually think of Wikipedia? We have mentioned its feeling of familiarity—those medical students we mentioned complimented Wikipedia for "usefulness", even though they did not find it particularly reliable. And a disturbing paradox is at work. On the one hand, Wikipedia prides itself on its "democratic" credentials: the whole world's knowledge at your fingertips. But on the other, Wikipedia contrives to exude a monolithic sense of authority. Even the identity of its multitude of contributors lies cloaked in anonymity. Any debate or conflict between contributors takes place on a discreet "talk page", away from public attention. The sense of authority is buttressed by a sober, scholarly layout, replete with academic-looking footnotes and references. This is how ordinary users may be compensating for lack of expertise, according to a 2011 study of 347 users asked to read Wikipedia articles on car engines (Lucassen & Schraagen, 2011).

We may go to Wikipedia to know, but we come away with something further. To "know", on Planet Wikipedia, is not just to possess knowledge but to know what it is that the world knows—indeed, to "know" the world. In some ways, Wikipedia is a social experience. It gives a sense of mass participation. Everyone, it would seem, is using it. While this does not generally allow you to get personal, it certainly allows you an experience of the crowd (Malone, Laubacher & Dellarocas, 2010)—not unlike watching a YouTube channel or reading Amazon reader reviews. In some ways, then, Wikipedia is part of the social media, or Web 2.0.

Thus it is no surprise that, while teachers and students have their reservations about Wikipedia (Kubiszewski, Noordewier, & Costanza, 2011), the general public appears to have few qualms. There has been a general shift of preferences among Internet users from reliability and accuracy of information to availability and easy searchability, and Wikipedia has benefited.

What, finally, does the public think about Wikipedia as a source of health information? It is difficult to say. In 2009, two administrators of English Wikipedia observed: "Despite several calls to adopt the principles that underlie its success, there is virtually no research on Wikipedia's role as a source of health information" (Laurent & Vickers, 2009). At time of writing, surveying English-language published research, this still appears to be the case.

Wikipedia Prescription Drug Pages

We conducted a broad sweep of the Wikipedia articles for the generic of America's 30 best-selling prescription drugs of 2009, and then subjected four of these articles to a detailed inspection. Here are our most significant findings.

General Profile

Format

The prescription drug pages followed a general Wikipedia style:

> clear and uncluttered format
> prominent list of contents
> uniform font and heading system
> "classic" three-column page layout
> broad unbroken horizontal and vertical sweep

This was all quite encouraging. A format of this kind makes for easy reading; users will also benefit from the uniformity across entries.

No ads were allowed. In fact, the only link to brand or promotional content were the few external links tucked away at the foot of the page. In all these ways, Wikipedia shines among other drug portals and all the brand sites with their ads and plugs and their cluttered, unpredictable format.

Content

Wikipedia left plenty to be desired. These articles had no cautions or directives. Conspicuously absent were:

- what precautions to take
- how to take the medicine
- how to act if there are side effects, a missed dose or an overdose
- how to store it.

Neither were there any *implied* directives, of the kind "FDA recommends contacting a physician immediately for any of the following side effects".

There were still other, unpredictable gaps. Thus, in the article on *Adalimumab* (Humira), the section *Safety*, described as based on the product labeling, did not list the serious and most common side effects, but instead restricted itself to some serious and rare side effects and the FDA Black Box warning. There was no mention of precautions, contra-indications, interactions, dosage or overdose. Moreover, half of the content concerned historical topics of no immediate relevance to the patient.

Wikipedia articles, as a matter of policy, do not define a target audience, such as "patients" or "health care providers". Nor is it Wikipedia policy to signal the technical level of articles, let alone to pitch articles at any particular level of expertise or simplicity. In fact, some of the language we found was thoroughly technical. Take "The primary uses of Atorvastatin is for the treatment of dyslipidemia" or the *Drug Interactions* section at *Rabeprazole*:

> Rabeprazole decreases the concentration of ketoconazole in the plasma (in 33%), increases the concentration of digoxin (in 22%), and does not interact with liquid antacids. Rabeprazole is compatible with any medicine metabolized by the CYP450 (theophylline, warfarin, diazepam, phenytoin).

Users need to be fully aware of this before tackling an article.

All of this makes a Wikipedia drug page quite different from a patient information leaflet or a consumer drug portal.

Self-Presentation and Quality Control

Authorship, edits and oversight were, of course, anonymous. This is Wikipedia policy. It was not much different at many other sites we visited. However, on occasion there was an external link to some authoritative sources. In the case of Atorvastatin, it was:

1. MedlinePlus Drug information
2. U.S. National Library of Medicine: Drug Information Portal—Atorvastatin

Of the generic pages for the 10 best-selling US drugs of 2009, eight had an external link to the US National Library of Medicine and one to MedicineNet.

Surprisingly, of the generic pages for the 30 best-selling US drugs of 2009, six (as of May 15, 2011) were posting an editor's alert about shortcomings, primarily about paucity of citations. This may damage trust in the entries. Here are two examples:

Infliximab (Remicade)

> This article may require cleanup to meet Wikipedia's quality standards. (*January 2010*)

Duloxetine (Cymbalta)

> An editor has expressed a concern that this article lends undue weight to certain ideas, incidents, controversies or matters relative to the article subject as a whole. Please help to create a more balanced presentation. Discuss and resolve this issue before removing this message. (*March 2011*)

Summary

Wikipedia prescription drug articles are of some limited practical value to a patient or interested consumer:

1. On the one hand, they showed commendable clarity of format and freedom from distracting promotions.
2. On the other hand, many important elements of information were lacking, what was provided was frequently quite technical, there was no attempt to caution or advise—and, on top of this, there was no immediate indication to users that this was the kind of article they had arrived at.

If one then decided to look elsewhere, the only pointer we could find on these pages was through an external link to a drug portal. Unfortunately, we found these on some but not all the Wikipedia pages we visited. It may be time for a policy review.

CHAPTER EIGHT

A Prescription for Change

We began this investigation with very little hard evidence for how the average American uses the World Wide Web for prescription drug information and how he or she feels about it. The profiles in the preceding chapters provide rich evidence as to what is going on—and what should be done about it. We went for both depth and breadth: we sampled a wide range of websites which Americans are known commonly to visit for prescription drug information.

In many cases, it was abundantly clear how a user would interpret the information, and no extrinsic survey evidence was needed. (In fact, surveys themselves often raise questions of interpretation, as well as imposing severe limitations on the number of questions one asks).

What we found was a recurrent set of problems. Although some sites were better than others, there was a pattern of serious failings in form and content that may be endemic. Here are the more egregious:

INTELLIGIBILITY AND OTHER ISSUES OF USABILITY

- Important content was often marred by long and unwieldy sentences and paragraphs. This not only slows reading and impedes the search for key information but also has an intimidatory effect, particularly on poor readers and the visually challenged.

- The logical flow was often not immediately clear. Unfortunately, it may take a sharp editor to detect this and fix it.
- Urgent information (serious side effects, overdoses) was rarely highlighted and sometimes difficult to locate. In some cases, it was set in running text instead of in a bulleted list.
- Actionable items in general (such as dosage and storage) were rarely flagged for special attention, even though many or most users need a prompt of some sort.
- Textual or visual distractions (which includes outside links) commonly intervened in or jostled important content. In some cases, they even predominated over the drug information.
- Many websites, particularly the more heavily sponsored ones, suffered from clutter and poor organization, with frequent duplication and poorly titled or misleading links. A menu or a small link to a site map is no substitute for a prominent list of contents.

CREDIBILITY

- Indication of accreditation, ongoing oversight and responsibility for medical content was rarely displayed prominently on the main drug page. Where accreditation or sources of information were indicated, further details and contact information were rarely provided.

TRANSPARENCY AND PROBITY

- Ads and sponsored content were often not labeled clearly and legibly as such and could easily be mistaken for information. In particular, sponsored links often failed to make it clear that they were promoting a brand. Entire sponsored pages were sometimes not marked prominently as such at the top of the page.
- There was often inadequate visual "fencing" between ads and information.
- The result was frequently a hybrid of information and promotion.

ADVISORIES TO CONSULT A HEALTH CARE PROFESSIONAL

- There was rarely a prominent message to tell your doctor about any other medications you are taking.
- There was rarely a prominent message to speak to your pharmacist. For most people today, their local pharmacist is by far the most accessible source of expert drug information.

The inescapable conclusion is that the informational content at prescription drug information sites is frequently hard to absorb and hard to use. This is particularly so for the less-literate and the elderly. But this is more than a cognitive mess. There were also serious challenges to transparency and trust. And we found too little direct evidence of the "deep content" and editorial imagination that information organizations like to promise us.

Later in this chapter, we offer a collated set of recommendations, many of them framed to target the deficiencies we have identified.

How can such flaws have come about? Some appear to indicate that whoever it is that is tailoring the FDA-approved prescribing information to the ordinary user, there is a pervasive lack of linguistic and formatting skills and a failure to appreciate how people need to use them. Some of these flaws are surely the work of a rampant culture of commercialism that continues to subvert the pharmaceutical industry's declared commitment to codes of practice, and which the FDA is unable or unwilling to check.

The design and content departments that produced these pages must bear much of the responsibility. So too must the regulators and the accreditation bodies that failed to monitor it all. The FDA has long recognized some of these deficiencies and it already possesses the regulatory powers to do something about them—and yet it routinely laments that more experimental studies are needed. It is almost comical (if it were not so grave) that the FDA has for years been sanctioning pages of dense mouse print for the summaries of risk information in magazine ads, as well as hundreds of tactical distractions in TV drug ads, and yet now all of a sudden it piously hits drug companies with warning letters about poor formatting (for example, Food and Drug Administration (2007) Warning Letter to Levulan Kerastick).

To the FDA's shame, there already exist a set of guidelines for general advertising on the Web, published by the Federal Trade Commission as long ago as 2000. These include such self-evident recommendations as:

- Use text or visual cues to encourage consumers to scroll to a disclosure.
- Label the link to convey the importance, nature and relevance of the information it leads to.
- Using hyperlink styles consistently allows consumers to know when a link is available.
- Don't let other parts of an ad get in the way.

In the words of Marianne Udow-Phillips (2011):

...as a whole, there is nothing that the pharmaceutical industry is doing that isn't within the rules of what they are permitted to do. [...] What is extremely important, however, is for consumers to be aware when they are being marketed to and when they are getting impartial, unbiased information. Unfortunately, in today's world of searches on the web, that is not always clear. So, before taking medical advice verbatim from a website, it would be well to read the fine print about sponsors, advertisers, and conflict of interest policies enforced by the site. In other words, don't stop at researching your medical conditions: research your websites, too.

SO WHERE'S THE PANACEA?

We have no easy prescriptions for transforming prescription drug websites. Nor did we expect to find any when we embarked on this book. For a start, there are just so many stakeholders involved, many with extraordinarily powerful vested interests. There are also all the usual factors, such as money, abilities, and sheer inertia, that impede change in any field of endeavor.

We hold no brief for any advocacy group. If we did, we might simply ignore these inconvenient truths and hammer away at a message. Rather, we are academics, given to confronting the complexities of reality. We have also been able to train our lenses from very different angles: one of us from pharmacy and marketing—the natural, clinical, and social sciences—and the other of us from linguistics and communications, the humanities. From these and from other angles, we are aiming to strike a workable balance between the real and the ideal.

Though we cannot propose a panacea, we do see room for far-reaching improvements in the way drug information is purveyed on the World Wide Web, to the benefit of all the parties concerned. In this chapter, we shall set them out.

We had a further goal in mind in writing this book: To offer a helping hand to the millions of Americans (and others) who are using the Web in its present state for guidance about prescription drugs. To this we will come in chapter 9.

ETHICAL CONSIDERATIONS: IDEALS AND DILEMMAS

To achieve the best in health for the maximum number of people: this is a goal to which everyone in the health business would subscribe. Drug information must, therefore, be designed to achieve the best in health.

However, as we have seen, that is not as straightforward as it sounds. There is no single way to measure the best health results; indeed, how could there be, given how complex a matter health is? Thus, for example, if we choose to regard *disease awareness* as a major goal, we can applaud the advertising campaigns for drugs combating toenail fungus or sleep disorders. Whatever might be our reservations about advertising prescription drugs, these advertisements do help educate about the disease. On the other hand, we may prefer to condemn awareness raising for certain drugs if it means "medicalizing" a relatively harmless condition.

How is the "information" most easily noticed, best respected, and best digested? In sober tones and relatively technical language—and in full? Jazzed up, simplified—and in part? Some people may be more inclined to watch a drug ad or read a web page if it is full of healthy-looking actors or engaging graphics, but others will find these thoroughly distracting. Some patients will expect full disclosure, others will be spooked; should we give them just part of the picture?

Medical ethicists have not been of one mind on these matters. Most would hold that some degree of "paternalism" is necessary, these being risky decisions on which one's doctor is best equipped to advise. The question is: what degree of paternalism? The United States Supreme Court (1976), in a landmark case for drug advertising, held that people "will perceive their own interests if only they are well enough informed"—and that they can be trusted to comprehend truthful information (whether they are reasonable and well-educated citizens or unthinking and ignorant ones). We are not so sure. Defining "well enough informed" is hard enough. Achieving it has proven to be beyond the ability of the American health system and successive Food and Drug Administrations.

Should doctors just use their own judgment to select what information you see? Or should they try to work from your own values? Or first try to discuss your values with you (Farrell, 2003)? For some health educators and ethicists, however, your doctor is a partner, not an authority. Full disclosure of drug information is the key to empowerment, and empowerment is the holy grail. Others would argue that alternative values—such as public safety or personal contentment or legal liability—count for more or for just as much.

Concern for public safety is justifiably more important than anyone's "right" to information about unapproved uses of a drug. So too the concern to avoid legal liability. And there are many people who would like to exercise their right *not* to know about all the rare side effects and interactions that could come with their medication.

Could all these needs somehow be met on the World Wide Web? Could "different pages for different people" be a workable solution?

Perhaps. There are two issues here: (1) generating all these types of pages, and (2) figuring out how to get people to use them.

On the first matter, we are confident that there is a keen interest among those advocating for the vulnerable—older adults, the low-literate, non-English speakers—to produce prototype pages and to test them. The key is to get these things out there and gauge popular opinion in the raw, in the same way as with any commercial product, and *not* to dally with endless scientific tests and trials (in the way beloved of the FDA).

On the second: Again, we believe there is a rising tide of interest among older adults and the low-literate in this kind of solution. Search engines could certainly help direct people with different needs to different types of page. Icons could also play a role. Health educators and web page designers should gear up to address these matters as a priority.

Returning, though, to the larger question we asked: No, it would be naive to fancy that every stakeholder's needs could be met on the World Wide Web. Thus, we see no obvious way of squaring demands for full disclosure on the Web with the demands of certain other stakeholders. Regulators insist that certain off-label uses favored by many doctors must remain unpublicized, however common they may be. And the Pharma industry is just as insistent that the facts about a drug's effectiveness should not be publicized.

A DIZZY MIX OF NEW REALITIES

However, we have to keep coming back to three other factors that must be placed on the balance of the ethical and the practical: the special nature of the World Wide Web—its easy accessibility, its intricacies, its overwhelming scale. We have outlined this in an earlier chapter, and we also reflected on the workings of the search engines that make it all available. The Web takes with one hand what it gives with the other. It is so inclusive; yet it seems destined to accentuate the gaps between people and make the vulnerable even more marginal. It evokes empowerment but it creates a sense of powerlessness. It breathes trust, but it breeds suspicion. The World Wide Web is what Antony Giddens (1991) has dubbed "high modernity", at its most extreme.

How far the practical realities of the Web will allow for drug information to meet a minimal ethical bar will only become apparent when the stakeholders come together to seize that bar.

THE STAKEHOLDERS: GOALS AND RESPONSIBILITIES

Five sectors have a legitimate stake in drug information. We say "legitimate" in the sense that they may be taking such drugs, or else they owe (or feel they owe) a duty of care or diligence to those who are taking them:

- The public (patients, caregivers and others)
- The medical profession, health educators and patients' advocates
- Commercial information providers (notably: Google and its ilk, information vendors, "point-of-care communication" systems, Web portals)
- Drug manufacturers and marketers ("Biopharma")
- Policy makers: Lawmakers, regulators and the Courts

THE PUBLIC

The available research confirms what anyone would expect: patients are asking their doctors (in the brief time allowed them) about the **purpose** of the drug, **dosages, precautions to take,** and **side effects.** In fact, consumers want much more information on side effects than doctors.

That, then, is the essence of what they need to find online. Of course, most patients prefer to receive this information from their physicians or pharmacists, but more often than not they don't (Morris, Tabak, & Gondek, 1997; Stevenson, Cox, Britten, & Dundar, 2004; Svarstad, Bultman, & Mount, 2004). In a national survey conducted in 2011, patients reported that their chief source of information on disease was overwhelmingly physicians, followed by the Internet, then pharmacists and nurses, then the news media (Quintiles, 2011). Ads and social media hardly mattered. But what patients say and what they do can be very different.

The public's needs can also vary substantially. Here are some of the chief factors:

- Point in time in treatment: The questions a patient has about a medicine are often very different at the start of treatment than down the line.
- Type of drug: Long-term drugs often require a different kind of information than those for acute uses (such as antibiotics).
- Type of patient: Educational background and level of literacy require very different modes of presentation. For the elderly, legibility is an extra issue; so is the organization of the information.

For these reasons—and others—a patient or caregiver may sometimes wish to know just the basics and sometimes a great deal more. This is an age of information overload; some tell the FDA that the chief side effects are all they wish to know. Others, however, evince a sense of betrayal after suffering a devastating adverse event of which they were not adequately warned.

A Pharma Industry digital specialist recently summed it up aptly (Hoenig-Carlson, 2011): "Consumers don't need more information but the right information, at the right time." Fortunately, the World Wide Web, suitably finessed and targeted at different readerships, has the potential to offer the right information and at the right time.

There is also evidence that the American public would be more comfortable receiving their information from a Government-approved source. At an FDA Public Meeting on July 31, 2003 on Useful Written Prescription Drug Information for Consumers, many commented that there is no comparison between FDA-designed leaflets and a commercial leaflet stapled to a pharmacy's paper bag containing an amber vial.

THE MEDICAL PROFESSION, EDUCATORS AND ADVOCACY GROUPS

Attitudes of American physicians to written drug information in general for patients have ranged from dismissive to enthusiastic. When the FDA first proposed in 1979 that patient leaflets be required for all drugs, the medical profession issued a flat rejection. Only a doctor could give information and advice. Even when the FDA retreated to just 10 drugs, doctors said "No". In 1995, the AMA (American Medical Association, 2011) rejected fresh FDA proposals to require medication leaflets.

Similar and even stronger resentment was felt about drug advertising. After all, as a historian of drug promotion has put it, such advertising (though commonplace today) has "undermine[d] our most historic principles of disease management and professional relationships" (Pines, 1999)—above all the traditional mystique of the physician. At the Congressional hearings in 2008, AMA President-elect Nancy Nielsen still felt the need to declare (Nielsen, 2008): "Direct-to-consumer ads often portray drugs through rose-colored glasses by including more information about a drug's benefits than risks."

The AMA has reversed its negative stance on patient leaflets: Recommendations drawn up in 2011 call for official information sheets to accompany medications—and for clear definitions of what is essential information (American Medical Association, 2011). But the AMA has not gone beyond such generalities. Furthermore, it only wants such information to be available online for physicians, not for their patients.

Unlike physicians, pharmacists have been providing written information for many years. But there is widespread dissatisfaction with it—and with the lack of time for counseling patients, which could eliminate 50% of errors (Mayer, 2008). A quite separate issue is the activities of online pharmacies, which (among other questionable practices) reassure the users by minimizing the side effects (Levaggi, Orizio, Domenighini, Bressanelli, Schulz, Zani, Caimi, & Gelatti, 2009). The FDA has criticized them as a public health risk, and we cannot regard them as a legitimate stakeholder in online information.

Consumer groups have had mixed feelings about drug advertising. When TV drug promotion began in the U.S., the National Consumers League spoke in favor: it would encourage consumers to communicate with their physicians and make them feel a little empowered. But the Consumer Federation of America and the powerful American Association of Retired Persons (AARP) were strongly opposed (Kolata, 1983). In May 2008, the AARP submitted testimony that called on a reluctant Congress to impose a two-year ban on the advertising of new drugs and a requirement that all drug ads be pre-vetted by the FDA.

More written drug information has been a major theme of The National Council on Patient Information and Education (NCPIE). It has pushed for the development of leaflets by pharmacy chains but wants them to be shorter and simpler. However, NCPIE has not so far issued any opinions about Web-based information or about any of the specific issues we have raised in this book.

By contrast, the Healthy People consortium takes specific positions on Web-based information. In its *Topics and Objectives for Healthy People 2020*, it sets two targets for "quality, health-related websites" (Healthy People, 2013):

- More disclosure of reliability
- Increased acceptance of established usability standards

The first target draws on a useful set of criteria created by the Office of Disease Prevention and Health Promotion (ODPHP): health websites should strive to

- identify the person/organization responsible for the site
- state the purpose and limitations of the site
- distinguish clearly between promotional and non-promotional content
- allow user feedback
- give a date of creation, update and review
- state a user and privacy policy

A proposal for better drug labels for seniors, by the California Gray Panthers, could help towards Web pages for seniors (Senate Health Committee Analysis, 2010). Here are some of their ideas:

- A color picture of the drug in addition to any textual description
- Directions for use printed in a bold, 14 pt font and in a position of prominence

- Warnings in another color than other instructions and using a small universal warning sign (circle with a slash across it). Warnings should include "severe reactions possible, serious food or alcohol interactions, possible dangers"

COMMERCIAL PROVIDERS OF DRUG INFORMATION

Commercial delivery of drug information comes in a wide variety of forms and functions: there are the traditional information vendors and pharmacy chains who use the official prescribing information and post-launch feedback to produce the pages for patients to read; the sophisticated "point-of-care communication" systems that offer personalized, targeted messages with your prescription, to educate you, remind you and follow you (while endearing you to a brand); the commercial drug portals with their various blends of facts and ads; and there are the Googles of this world, which pay their way by smart (some would say, sneaky) advertising.

One communications issue that divides point-of-care communicators is how tightly to interpret the regulations and FDA signals. Some tailor their drug information to their lawyers; others are educators at heart. As one executive told us,

> I would love to demonstrate that patients are better equipped to achieve positive health outcomes when manufacturers produce communications that emphasize health literacy and avoid information overload rather than enforce lockstep interpretation of legal/regulatory guidance.

Google is a powerful player in online drug information. Some of its actions seem to be designed to protect the public from an excess of commercialization—while at the same time protecting its own commercial interests. Google's life-blood is the advertising revenue stream that pumps the search results. We referred earlier to the sparkling non-profit PubMed Health link that Google requires to top the prescription drug results. We also wondered if there is a covert Google policy to limit (or even exclude) branded sites from the "organic" search results for brands and medical conditions. A third, verifiable Google concern is how to ensure that links to brands include enough risk information to stay on the right side of the law. In late 2009, after consultations with the FDA, Google unveiled proposals for new "standard" links. These would include a fixed warning (about contraindications and the like) and a link to additional risk information (Google, 2009). It would now be up to the advertisers to work with Google on a beta program.

MANUFACTURERS AND MARKETERS

Drug companies exist to produce drugs that help people, to increase market share and share price, and to maximize profit. The prime goal of the marketing division is to promote the drug to the consumer and to the physician. Marketing prescription drugs to the consumer has by now been enshrined in law for a generation.

The Industry wears its conscience on its sleeve. Americans should not think that "education is good, promotion is bad," in the words of John Kamp, former director of the American Association of Advertising Agencies. "Good education is marketing. Marketing [can] shorten the development cycle and get drugs out in the marketplace sooner" (Kamp, 2003).

Companies have not been shy to promote their drugs. The fact that such promotion was previously absolutely prohibited (and still is, except in the US and New Zealand) has not held them back in the slightest. Brand managers seek to exploit any and every loophole—while jealously watching their competitors and reporting them to the FDA for any infringement. One favored strategy is sponsorship, by which companies can boost their name without being held accountable for content, a practice that is beginning to attract the attention of regulators. Only occasionally has a company broken rank and put education ahead of promotion in its campaigns. Under extreme criticism in Congress in 2008, four major companies agreed to a six-month moratorium on new drug advertising and discontinued certain deceptive advertising practices, but weathered pressure for any other changes (Goldstein, 2008).

As the mass media migrate steadily from the networks and the press to the Internet, and as mass marketing morphs into niche marketing and, by virtue of digital technology, into small-group or individual targeting, the general style of promotion has been shifting: from the hard or soft sell to the invisible sell. Pharma marketers now chorus a new credo: The prime goal is to "engage" consumers, to open up channels, to listen, in short to "befriend" them.

A favored method of engagement and befriending is education. Companies have long been permitted to increase name recognition by sponsoring educational TV spots. Now, more and more company-sponsored websites are being devoted to a particular disease or condition. Ostensibly, sites such as LivingWithEpilepsy.com or ParkinsonsHealth.com are designed as educational sites, where individuals can share their experiences,. However, the consumer organization *Center for Digital Democracy* has warned that they are also "useful to pharmaceutical companies as a 'soft sell' opportunity, free of FDA-mandated risk-disclosure and other advertising requirements."

This does not mean that marketers are running amok. The social media are still uncharted territory, where marketers tend to act prudently. Running afoul of the FDA can entail a heavy price. Companies do throw ideas into the ring. Thus, Novartis suggested that a disease or product awareness message could include alert tags such as #[disease state], #[usonly] and #[blackbox] (Novartis, 2010). But by the time such ideas have been pondered and tested, the circus has often moved on.

THE FDA, CONGRESS AND THE COURTS

Looming over all the other American stakeholders in drug information is Congress—and what happens to the laws it legislates when the FDA attempts to cloak them in flesh and sinews or, on occasion, ends up being taken to the Courts and falling foul of the First Amendment.

However, Congress itself has done little to change the status quo on prescription drug promotion and information (and shows little will to do so). Nor indeed has the White House. The very occasional hearings and investigations that have flamed up have fizzled out.

The lobbying power of some of the other stakeholders can be irresistible. At times, the hand of the White House itself has been sensed pulling on the reins at the FDA. Principles and ideals perish regularly on Capitol Hill and at the FDA in the mire of political compromise, posturing and expediency.

Over the years, the struggle between more regulation and less regulation of drug information has surged this way and that. The Supreme Court has increasingly questioned the FDA's blanket right to shut down an advertisement in the name of truth and safety. Commercial freedom of speech is to be jealously protected. The courts have also persuaded the FDA that it should be thinking of how a reasonable educated consumer would react rather than thinking of protecting the ignorant and vulnerable (Carver, 2008). And where, once, one might have had some hope of suing for harm caused by drug information under stricter state laws, the FDA has now been insisting that its own regulations pre-empt the laws of any state (Hall, 2009).

All in all, however, the basic system remains intact. Let us then sum up the current state of play at the FDA:

1. The FDA is acutely aware that its powers are limited and liable to legal challenge, and its manpower meager. It has thus preferred persuasion and guidance over regulation. Many accusations of FDA inaction or ineptitude are best directed elsewhere. The *Prescription Drug User Fee Act* (PD-UFA) (Food and Drug Administration, 2012b) called for drug companies to pay $11 million to enable the FDA to review every commercial. Many companies consented. But Congresswoman Rosa DeLauro refused to

allow that money to be transferred to the FDA budget, and that was that (Barlas, 2008).

2. Since the early eighties, when companies began advertising prescription drugs to the public, the FDA has tried to walk a tight-rope between the pressures of the pharmaceutical industry, the healthcare professions, the consumer and the Courts, proclaiming : "Direct-to-consumer advertising is not inherently bad or good. It can be useful or harmful, depending on how it's done" (Ostrove, 1998 cited by Nordenberg, 1998).

3. All such advertising is meant, by law, to provide (1) full consumer-friendly disclosure of information about a drug, and (2) a "fair balance" between information on the benefits and on the risks.

4. For printed ads, the FDA interprets the law of full disclosure as requiring a so-called "brief summary" of consumer information. In reality, however, this is a long, dense page of obscure information in miniscule type. This must rank as one of the most bizarre provisions the FDA has ever made in the name of information for consumers.

5. For TV and radio ads to meet the requirements of full disclosure, the FDA came up with another "stretch", with the goal of satisfying Industry's hunger for drug advertising on radio and TV. The "solution" was that only the main risk information would appear briefly in the ad, while the full information could be provided somewhere else, by mail/phone/fax etc. This set a precedent for the websites of today, where the "safety information" is often out of sight until you scroll down or run a search for it.

6. Is there really "Fair balance" between benefits and risks if the benefits are laced with catchy tunes and pretty pictures, sometimes timed to distract from the warnings? The FDA has had to struggle with its conscience—and this struggle continues. Back in 1997, after evaluating the first broadcast ads, the FDA noted gravely that "careful consideration must be given to the context in which the safety information is presented. Any attempts to trivialize important safety information would be misleading." Occasionally, the FDA has held hearings, announced some new evidence, and sent out warning letters. Most recently, in 2010, it issued a "proposed rule" for making key information in TV and radio ads user-friendly and free of distraction. Nevertheless, it has largely preferred to turn a blind eye. Congressional hearings in 2008 confirmed this—and the General Accounting Office has spoken darkly of foot-dragging in FDA pursuit of rogue advertising that seems to have the fingerprints of the Bush White House all over it. More important to keep the Pharma industry content than to uphold the spirit of the law. This, too, has set a precedent for websites today.

7. Using legal discretion, the FDA has not required ads to disclose how effective a drug has been proven to be; nor to mention that there may exist other drugs of that type.

8. The big bang of the 2008 Congressional hearings on drug advertising has faded. Some Pharma giants said sorry, pulled some ads and announced a brief moratorium, but it now seems to be "business as usual."

9. As regards medication leaflets, the FDA is more or less shut out of the picture. It has no role in specifying what content is most relevant to patients (except for the handful of Medication Guides) and only offers unenforced guidelines on formatting (Shrank & Avorn, 2007). "Drug Facts" labels are not required for prescription drugs.

10. The World Wide Web is a headache for the enforcers at the FDA. They insist that it is just a huge hybrid of print and broadcasting, and so have shied away from issuing any special guidelines. And yet the FDA does appear to harbor some special standards for the Web in its regulatory bosom—to judge by the warning letters it sends out to companies. First, there appeared to be a "one-click rule" for search ads: as long as the risk information was one click away from the ad, all was well. And then, in 2009, the FDA warned that all was *not* well: The risks now had to be listed on the same web page as the pleasant stuff. It also appeared that the FDA was at last turning its attention to that ubiquitous cog of our virtual reality, the link—and requiring that basic risk information appear there as well. But how well the FDA really understands the complex communicative workings of a website is not at all clear.

11. Many other issues raised by the Web remain unresolved. Thus, prescription advertising and labeling have to be submitted to FDA for approval after they have been first aired. But how is a product home page to be submitted? Indeed, are product home pages to be considered consumer promotions? Should "fair balance" apply to every page (Reichertz, 1996)?

HOW WE WOULD TRANSFORM DRUG INFORMATION WEBSITES

We are addressing these proposals, collated and consolidated, to writers, website designers, legal departments, brand managers and regulators alike. They all contribute to the online drug information we have been evaluating.

This mix of contributors has to achieve a modicum of collaboration for this to work. In particular, regulators and the Pharma industry must urgently pool ideas and negotiate objectives to create Internet-specific standards for brand websites.

We recognize that some sites are sponsored and some not, which is bound to make some difference in appearance. Nonetheless, much of what we propose here should apply to any and every website.

In all that follows, one thing has been uppermost in our mind: how are drug information websites actually used? Clearly, people use them to locate information—and often they need to absorb it but sometimes they just need to know it exists, often they will want to remember it and very frequently they will want to act on it, sometimes they bookmark it or refer back to it, and there are times when they print it out.

CONTENT

1. Doctors, pharmacists and consumer groups have long warned that written information is only a back-up to the information that really counts: the advice given by your health care professional. Drug sites should therefore carry a prominent message "Speak to your pharmacist".
2. Any claims relating to the benefits and performance of a specific drug should ideally include comparisons with taking a placebo. However, we are aware that industry has long been resistant to this and regulators have complied.
3. We found scant reference in drug sites to sources. While most medical sources may be meaningless to the average user, some can definitely help decision making in concert with one's personal physician. To quote from the HON Code of Conduct for medical and health websites:

> Where appropriate, information contained on this site will be supported by clear references to source data and, where possible, have specific HTML links to that data.

4. The date when a clinical page was last modified must be clearly displayed (e.g. at the bottom of the page).

OVERSIGHT

1. Drug information sites can seem like an onion, with many layers of safeguard—oversight, accreditation, responsibility. The public deserve to know what these safeguards are all about, and when they are absent.
2. Who provides oversight and who bears responsibility for medical content should be stated prominently. Providing the name of a person or

organization is not enough; the public has a right to information about qualifications or activities, and a contact address.

3. Any accreditation logos should appear at the top of the home page, so that users gain an immediate sense of a site's reliability. The significance of such accreditation should be indicated right there, with the date of accreditation and when the page was last monitored.

4. It is widely believed that the FDA vets all professional-sounding drug information. Unfortunately, this is far from the truth. If portions of a site are under FDA "sponsorship" or "partnership", there should be a prominent statement that the site as a whole is not under FDA oversight.

ORGANIZATION

1. Authoritative content should be reviewed as carefully for style and coherence as it would be for scientific accuracy.

2. The format and organization of content at MedlinePlus is, in many ways, a model for drug portals to follow. There are no textual or visual distractions whatsoever: no other topics breaking up the flow, no links—except the navigationally necessary *Return to top*—and no ads.

3. The most important thing about a message is what we want to *do* about it. For drug information, it is vital to distinguish between actionable and "background" information, and between urgent and non-urgent. Visitors to drug sites should be able to tell immediately where to go.

   Thus, side effects should be presented as a bulleted list, rather than in narrative form A clear distinction should be made between the urgent and non-urgent side effects. Actionable side effects should be highlighted. Similarly, Dosage and Storage sections should be clearly flagged.

4. Drug content must predominate at a drug information page. Taking drugs is a serious business, which is why the laws governing commercial drug information are so much more stringent than those for, say, furniture or toys. If ads or other distracting content are allowed to dominate, it can only trivialize the information, as well as making it harder to locate. A general quality criterion governing any kind of information site is especially important here: Avoid clutter.

5. Ads on health websites must be prominently labeled as such. The word "advertisement" in miniscule letters is quite inadequate. There must also be clear visual "fencing" of ads, so that they are not confusable with information content. The need to distinguish advertisements from educational

content has never been so acute as today, when the advertising industry is engaged in reinventing itself as the consumer's best friend and confidant—and employing a host of new and bewildering tactics to mask its advertising persona, such as smuggling itself into the social media.

6. Sponsorship is typically just a more subtle attempt to promote a brand, by mentioning it or alluding to it. What we have said about advertising applies with even more force to sponsorship. So any sponsorship lines must be displayed prominently at the top of the page, while making clear which content is not sponsored.

7. Sponsored content can run the gamut from advertising to information, and it should be transparent what its purpose really is. Websites by nature subject the user to tricky navigational choices at links that are often less than transparent. Drug sites should make it clear at the link whether a sponsored link is going to bring one to a site that is strongly branded or not. Not to make this clear is an imposition on the user and often worse.

8. Coherence is crucial: Content must flow in a logical manner. It must also be signposted with well-phrased headings and introductory sentences.

   Navigational links themselves must be organized logically. Readers must always know where they are and where they're going. Duplication of content should be avoided; it is extraordinarily bewildering.

9. Emergency information (serious side effects, overdoses) should be highlighted and easy to locate from the first screen you land at. Designers should develop standardized methods for foregrounding urgent warnings, e.g. bullets and/or bolding, upper case. Similarly, standard graphics (color-coding?) should be developed for distinguishing the three levels of action "Get emergency help", "Call doctor at once", "Less serious side effects".

   Drug sites should develop a standard prominent line to call one's doctor and/or one's pharmacist for medical advice about side effects, and two standard warnings, to be displayed prominently high up on the home page and on all individual drug pages, (a) to tell your doctor about any other meds you're taking and (b) not to start any new med without telling your doctor.

10. One major use of consumer information pages is to provide "take-aways" that users can easily memorize and refer back to. To this end, designers and usability experts should test furnishing a page or an area of a page with a "memory box" containing 1–2 word prompts.

11. Pages profiling a medication should place all information on the function and use of that drug in an uninterrupted visual flow, segregating other information (e.g. other drugs in the same class) into a separate flow.

12. Searching within a site should be extremely simple. Drug sites should provide prominently (a) a list of contents, and (b) a link to a site map. Ideally, both of these should be located at a standardized place on the page, marked by a standardized symbol or logo. This is one of many tasks for Pharma web designers to address as a group, in consultation with usability and literacy specialists.

13. Easy printability is as critical as searchability. Printing can be made so much more easy if a customized printing version is made available. Ideally, this should omit advertisements—in the same way as it is possible to record from television without including the commercials. Easy printing is of particular importance for older adults.

LANGUAGE

1. Sentences and paragraphs must be kept to a moderate length. Long sentences or convoluted syntax may be acceptable in academic prose but the average reader today finds them tedious and hard to digest.

2. It is surprising how often readers fail to get a writer's point. Writers should return at intervals to what they have written, to ensure that they made their point clearly. This kind of clarity is not the sort of thing that can be mechanically monitored with a check list—it requires a *feel* for what's clear and what isn't. And of special importance for online information: Writers need to check that what they wrote hasn't been mangled or subtly distorted by all the cuts and splices that go into building a web page.

3. Medicine and medical people breed medicalese. They are so inured to it that it never occurs to them that there could be a problem. So it takes unremitting effort by style-minders to keep it at bay. Sometimes, the simplest seeming language is a trap. We have noted the problems with something like *Take two tablets by mouth twice daily* and how much better it would be to say *Take 2 tablets by mouth at 8 in the morning, and take 2 tablets at 9 at night.* More research is desperately needed into misunderstandings and solutions.

4. Simplified versions of key pages should be feasible to open up websites to many more groups of users. This would include simplified style, vocabulary, glossaries, simpler formats such as Q & As and short take-aways. Far too little has been achieved in this area, but a concerted effort could yield modules and various solutions that could be shared across many kinds of site.

5. Older adults are an expanding slice of online America but they have been poorly served. We have made little mention of them thus far, for the unfortunate reason that the drug websites we have been critiquing have themselves made little mention of them. Nor have regulators or other stakeholders. Research has underlined that when older adults fail to take their medications correctly, it is often because they lack the necessary information, which in turn often comes down to inadequate instructions. Some progress has been made in the last few years towards developing patient-centered instructions for older adults that are an improvement on some of the more usual pharmacy leaflets (Morrow, Weiner, Young, Steinley, Deer, & Murray, 2005). This involves large print, simple language, icons, and an order of presentation suited to the way older adults think about taking their meds (their "mental schema"): First, the purpose of the meds; second, the way to take them; third, possible outcomes such as side effects.

6. Spanish and other major minority languages in the U.S. could also be catered for, at least by providing basic glossaries. For speakers of Spanish or French, use might also be made of drug information developed for Latin American and Francophone markets.

At the end of the day, however well judged the content and however careful the oversight, drug information succeeds or falls by the quality of its organization and language. Achieving clarity and coherence is an art. It is not to be left to technical experts or to website designers. It can only be entrusted to highly skilled writers with a holistic understanding of how a website works.

More important even than highly skilled writers, a drug site must have a guiding hand—someone who sees the whole picture. It cannot be emphasized enough that, for many users, visiting a website is a rough passage. They are pitched from page to page, often uncertain where they are going, and it needs a designer with a sense of the whole to make this a safe experience.

CHAPTER NINE

How to Use a Prescription Drug Website

So far, we have described how prescription drugs have been promoted directly to consumers, how prescription drug websites have been designed, how the FDA and other stakeholders function, and how prescription drug websites could be transformed to be more informative, balanced, and useful for consumers. In this chapter, we give some practical advice for how consumers can evaluate and use prescription drug websites for becoming more informed and for making decisions about their health care.

KNOW YOURSELF

Our first suggestion is to know yourself. How do you like to obtain information? How do you like to make decisions? How involved do you want to be in making decisions about your health? How have you been vulnerable to making decisions that you later realized might not have been the best ones? We propose that the more you know about yourself when it comes to processing information and making decisions, the better off you will be when it comes to looking at prescription drug websites and when it comes to talking about prescription drugs with others.

Most people want to make the best decisions in their lives but with the minimum amount of effort. There are some decisions that we make based on what we've done in the past. For example, if you buy a certain brand of breakfast cereal and like it, you may continue to buy that brand over and over again out of habit. However, there are other decisions that we make only after very careful information gathering and decision making. If you are married, think about how long you knew your spouse and how much you learned about him or her before you decided to get married. Choosing a spouse to marry, or a house to purchase, or even the type of car to drive, typically takes much more time and effort than other routine decisions such as buying a box of breakfast cereal. The point is, there are some things for which we willing to invest a lot of time in processing information and making decisions. There are other things for which we are not willing to invest much time.

When it comes to prescription drugs, not everyone views them the same way. For some, a great deal of effort is invested into learning about and using the very best medicines for their unique situation. Others would rather not think about using medicines at all and, when they need one, will use it as directed with no questions asked.

So where are you in this regard? How important is information about prescription drugs to your specific situation? Even if medicines are not that vital to your well-being now, what would you do if you developed an ailment that needed prescription drug therapy? Almost all of us have used or will need to use a prescription drug at some time in our lives. According to Kemper & Metter (2002), having the right information, in the right amount, and at the right time is as important to getting better as a medication, a lab test, or even a surgical procedure. Information guides our decisions and changes our behaviors. With good information patients can often heal themselves. Without it, they can do themselves harm, overlook effective cures, and undermine the best-laid clinical plans (Kemper & Metter, 2002).

If you take time to conduct a self-assessment about (1) what type of health consumer you are, (2) how you process information, and (3) how you make decisions, you will not only help yourself in knowing what to look for and how to use a prescription drug website, but also can share this information with others (physicians, pharmacists) to help them know how to best communicate with you and make decisions for you and with you. Here are a few things to consider:

1. What Type of Health Care Consumer are You?

As mentioned in Chapter 1, White, Draves, Soong, and Moore (2004) identified and described four health care consumer segments. If you think about the segment that you are in, you can gain perspective about how common or unique you are in the overall population. As you consult prescription drug websites, you can consider if the information was designed with your segment in mind or perhaps it was designed for another one. Looking at information this way can help you judge the extent to which the information really applies to your situation. If the information doesn't apply very well, then it would be best to consult other sources of information or to seek the advice of an expert.

Thinking about what segment you are in also can help you interact with health care professionals such as physicians and pharmacists. Health professionals serve many people with similar needs and conditions. After a while, they may start treating everyone with the same condition or treatment in a similar way. As a patient, the more you can open the eyes of your health professionals to your unique needs, wants, and characteristics, the better they can tailor treatments and information to meet you where you are at.

Recall that White and his colleagues described the four segments as:

- "The Healthy Half"—the 51% of the adult population who have no obvious health problems and consider themselves to be in excellent health. They have little interest in health information from any source and are largely immune to commercial messages.
- "The Doctor Led"—the 28% who tend to have lifestyle-restricting conditions and are receptive to the messages in drug advertisements. Although they often discuss advertised medicines with their doctors, they unfailingly defer to their physician's judgment and advice, using only those treatments that their doctor prescribes. Individuals in this group are likely to be reminded by advertising to refill an existing prescription or to resume treatment.
- "The Self-Managers"—the 13% who report above-average health, and whose complaints tend to be occasional or seasonal. This group tends to self-treat with over-the-counter medications. They are not particularly responsive to advertising or other health-related information.
- "The Solution Seekers"—the remaining 8% of U.S. adults who suffer from conditions that restrict their lifestyle, and who are receptive to advertising messages because they proactively seek new solutions to their health care wants and needs. They report below-average health and are more inclined than the other groups to take medicines to prevent symptoms rather than just treat symptoms of a disease and to respond to advertised messages about their conditions. In addition to using information from advertisements, they read health-related publications and use the Internet to research their conditions and possible treatments. After doing their homework, they discuss what they have learned with their physician and often ask to try a particular drug.

If you can identify yourself in one of these groups, you just learned a lot about yourself that you can use as you visit prescription drug websites and as you interact with health care professions. For example, what if you are in the "Healthy Half" but suddenly get diagnosed with a health problem that needs medication? As you go to websites to find information about the disease and treatment options, it would be helpful to acknowledge that you are a novice in these matters and could use expert help. As you interact with health professionals, they would appreciate knowing that you have been in the "Healthy Half" of the population and really don't know what to expect, how to find information, or how to make good decisions in this new area of your life. That information goes a long way in helping your health care team meet you where you are.

Here is another example. Suppose you are in the "Solution Seeker" segment. You have familiarity with your numerous health conditions, like to find information on your own, and want to be totally involved in your health care decision making. First, knowing that this may mean that you will get absorbed with all the information available on the Internet, you might need to budget your time wisely as you review this information. Second, sharing this information with your health care team will help them get ready for meetings with you and budget the time they need to go over your questions and ideas for treatment. They will appreciate the "heads up" and will be able to prepare for it!

How Do You Make Choices?

Choice among alternative courses of action lies at the heart of the decision-making process. The study of how people make preferential choices and judgments has been of great interest to psychologists, economists, and researchers in other fields (Payne, Bettman & Johnson, 1993; Chewning & Sleath, 1996). Research has shown that human decision behavior is highly sensitive to a wide variety of task and context factors. For example, the same individual often uses different processes for making choices rather than judgments, for choosing among few versus many alternatives, or for deciding among a set of good versus a set of bad options. Selection of an information processing strategy depends upon the particular decision problem.

Decision-making related to illness, health, and drug product selection is becoming more patient-centered. A patient-centered approach emphasizes patient priorities, allows the patient to co-define regimen selection with his or her prescriber, focuses on engagement between the patient and the prescriber, increases patient control over treatment, and enhances the patient's status in the prescriber-patient relationship. Direct-to-consumer advertising for prescription drugs can provide information upon which patients can make decisions about the therapy choice they prefer. The patient's choices might be different than his or her prescriber's and create conflict in the patient-prescriber relationship. As you consider information contained within a prescription drug website, we propose that it would be helpful if you knew about your preferred *information processing strategy* for making decisions. In addition, as you talk about this information with your health care provider, we also propose that it would be helpful to know about your preferred *decision making style* as you work with your health care providers for making prescription drug choices.

2. How Do You Process Information?

Information processing strategies vary depending on the context and situation. Decisions involve a trade off between accuracy and effort. It is likely that some individuals will find information contained in prescription drug websites very useful while others would prefer to depend upon their prescriber to make decisions on their behalf. It is possible that individuals will "self-select" for visiting prescription drug websites so that those who will value the information will most likely visit those sites and those who will not value the information won't bother to go to the websites. However, the Internet and social network sites are becoming so common, it is likely that most people will eventually use a prescription drug website at some time.

If you visit a prescription drug website for information, you should realize that you may process the information differently than you typically process other information. This could be due to your level of interest in the topic (level of involvement) or the extent to which you are feeling overwhelmed and overloaded by the information (information overload).

As you consider information contained in prescription drug websites, consider the following (Payne, Bettman, & Johnson, 1993):

- Are you being consistent or are you being selective when it comes to the amount of time you are spending on each alternative treatment option (i.e. various medications) or on each feature of the medications (e.g. benefits vs. risks)? If you are consistent, it means that you are processing information in a comparative way, weighing the advantages and disadvantages. If you are selective, it means that you are trying to eliminate alternatives or features and using just part of the information.
- How long are you spending on the information? Are you spending enough time to consider all options or just looking for information that will provide a suitable alternative to try?

- Are you focusing more on alternative treatment options (i.e. going to various prescription drug websites to check out all the alternatives) or are you focusing more on features of a particular treatment option (e.g. benefits, risks, costs)? Looking at features for a particular option before going on to any others takes less effort, but doesn't provide a full picture.
- Are you using a numbering system to tally the pluses and minuses of the treatment options or attributes? Or, are you using a gut feeling for making comparisons?
- How many alternatives are you considering? Just one medication? Or, all available treatment options?
- How many features are you considering? Just one feature (e.g. benefits)? Or, all sorts of features (e.g. benefits, side effects, risks, cost, convenience, access, insurance coverage)?
- How much time do you wish to devote to processing information to make a decision?
- Are you making this decision for yourself or someone else?
- Do you need to justify this decision to others?
- How much knowledge and experience do you have in this area?
- How important is it to you that you make the "most accurate" decision?
- Will this decision impact on other decisions that you will need to make in the future?
- Is processing information for this decision leading to information overload and causing you to feel overwhelmed?

By asking yourself these questions, you can take a step back and consider how useful a particular prescription drug website really is to you. If you find that you are becoming overwhelmed or overloaded, it might be a good time to step back and consider other options. These other options include:

- Changing information environments—the website is not the best source of information for you at this time. It might be time to use another source.
- You may need to consult other sources of information to define terms or learn more about what the website may have been referring to. You may ask another person to visit the website with you to talk about the information together and what it means.
- Training—before using the website, you may need to take time to enhance your knowledge regarding some of the things discussed at the site.
- Replacing the decision maker—if you are being overloaded by information and find the decision task too overwhelming, you may want to consult an expert such as a physician or pharmacist to help make the decision on your behalf.

3. How Do You Prefer to Make Decisions?

Your *decision making style* also would be helpful to know as you work with your health care providers for making prescription drug choices based on the information you find (Chewning & Sleath, 1996; Horne & Weinman, 2004; Gochman, 1997). Some consumers do a lot of research on their own, process the information completely, and come up with a course of action they would like to try. However, when it comes time to talk with their prescriber about receiving a prescription for the medication, the process falls apart. One reason for this happening is that patients and prescribers do not let each other know about their preferred decision making styles.

Here are three types of decision making styles to think about. If you can identify which you prefer and share that with your health care providers, you will have made great strides in improving communication and decision making with them. The three treatment decision making styles are: (1) paternalistic, (2) informed, and (3) shared.

The **paternalistic** treatment decision making style consists of a practitioner making the treatment decision on his or her own and then telling the patient about that decision using one-way communication, limited to a discussion of medical topics, with a minimum amount of information shared. The **informed** treatment decision making style is similar in that there is one way communication from the practitioner to the patient only about medical topics. However, in this style of decision making the practitioner shares all relevant medical information with the patient so that the patient can make the treatment decision on his or her own. This style is sometimes suggested by practitioners when the preferred treatment option depends on patients' personal priorities and the prescriber wants the patient to think about those personal things and then make the final choice.

The **shared** treatment decision making style involves two-way communication between the practitioner and patient in which both medical and personal information is shared. All relevant information is shared for decision making and the practitioner and patient make decisions collaboratively. An extension of shared decision making is called **concordance** (Horne & Weinman, 2004) which is "an agreement reached after negotiation between a patient and health care professional that respects the beliefs and wishes of the patient in determining whether, when and how medicines are to be taken. Although reciprocal, this is an alliance in which the health care professionals recognize the primacy of the patient's decisions about taking the recommended medications." In this style of decision making, the health care professional shares expertise and the patient shares goals for the treatment. Together, they try to come to agreement about the best option to follow. This style requires a lot of time and effort, but for very complicated or important decisions it is worth it.

More and more health care providers are being trained to consider the decision making styles of their patients. You may find that more recently trained practitioners are more open to a shared decision making style and practitioners trained longer ago may prefer the more traditional paternalistic style. As you share your preferred style with your health care practitioners, you may find that they have a preferred style for interacting with their patients. If your styles don't match, it might be a good idea to select another health care provider who can accommodate your preferred style.

In this section, we proposed that knowing yourself is a good first step for using a prescription drug website. If you know (1) what type of health care consumer you are, (2) how you process information, and (3) how you prefer to make decisions, you can then visit prescription drug websites with confidence in knowing when it is in your best interest to use the website and when it may be better to leave the website and get information and advice elsewhere. In the next section, we give some ideas for "knowing the source" of the information contained on the website.

KNOW THE SOURCE

Do you believe everything you read or hear? How do you determine what is trustworthy and credible and what is not? How can you tell if your perception of what you read or hear is the correct interpretation? Sometimes our minds play tricks on our thought process and we come to erroneous conclusions. Here are some fun examples to illustrate the point:

Ask a person to spell the word "SPOT" (s-p-o-t), then the word "TOPS" (t-o-p-s), and then the word "POTS" (p-o-t-s). Then say "Quick, what do you do at a green traffic signal?" Without hesitation, many people will say "Stop." Nope. You should "go" at a green traffic signal.

What do you put in a toaster? Toast! Nope. Bread goes in a toaster. Toast is what comes out.

What do cows drink? Milk! Wrong again. We get milk from cows. They typically drink water.

Here is one more example that is related to perception. Look at the FedEx logo that is commonly seen on delivery trucks, cargo planes, and packages. Can you see the arrow in the Fed Ex logo?

Hint: It is pointing to the right.
Hint: It is between the E and the x.
Hint: It is colored white when the letters are on a white background.

See it? Many people above the age of five can't see it right away since we tend to focus on the letters too much.

There are many other examples of how we can have error in our perception. When it comes to advertising in general, there is a great deal of effort given to creating the most persuasive messages rather than the most informative ones. The same holds true for prescription drug advertising. The goal of such promotion is to maximize the persuasive effect of the advertising while still complying with FDA guidelines.

We propose that a good way to evaluate prescription drug websites for credibility, trustworthiness, and usefulness for your needs is to compare the extent to which the websites focus on persuasion versus information.

Persuasion

One way to affect individuals' decision-making is through persuasion (Petty & Cacioppo, 1986; Schommer, Doucette, & Worley, 2001; Haugtvedt & Priester, 1997). There are two distinct routes to persuasion. The first route, called the central route, focuses on active thinking about the decision or the object-relevant information provided by messages. The second route, called the peripheral route, focuses more on cues that might be associated with the decision. These cues (such as the credibility of the source of the message, or rewards that may be associated with the message) are the primary means for persuasion. Persuasion theory suggests that the source of the message, how the message is presented, and characteristics of the recipient can affect how information is processed for decision-making. From this perspective, direct-to-consumer advertising for prescription drugs could quite easily lead to persuasion and changes in attitudes that are misleading or harmful through the use of carefully crafted cues in the ad. We outlined some of the potential for harm in previous chapters.

Related to persuasion is something called "attitude strength" in which strong attitudes should have a greater impact on judgments and decision-making than weak ones (Haugtvedt & Priester, 1997; Haugtvedt, Schumann, Schneier, & Warren, 1994; Haugtvedt & Wegener, 1994). Stronger attitudes, compared to weaker ones, will be (1) more persistent over time, (2) more resistant to counter-persuasion, and (3) more predictive of behavior. This view suggests that it is not only the *level* of favorable or unfavorable views towards an advertised product but also the persistence and resistance to counter persuasion that means the most for influencing behavior.

From an advertising perspective, favorable attitudes about an advertised product must persist all the way to the doctor's office, through the pharmacy, and all the way home to where the person will take the medication. Prescription drug websites are valuable tools for reinforcing attitudes about drug products so that people not only want the medication but also will continue to take it over long periods of time even when other alternatives become available.

A key component of persuasion is to convince an individual that a certain outcome will occur if a medication is taken as directed (Lau, 1997; Strecher, Champion, & Rosenstock, 1997; Reich, Erdal, & Zautra, 1997). This is called influencing the "outcome expectation." In addition, an individual needs to be persuaded that he or she can successfully enact the medication taking behavior (remembering to take the medication, continuing the medication even if side effects are experienced, etc.). This is called building "self-efficacy." In order to build outcome expectations and self-efficacy, advertising for prescription drugs often will incorporate role modeling (e.g. showing actors getting relief by taking the medication) and reinforcement of behaviors (e.g. through the use of verbal or visual cues). Prescription drug websites are especially amenable to role modeling and reinforcement of behaviors since they are not limited by a 30 second or 60 second broadcast commercial time limit. Also, websites can use video, graphics, hyperlinks and other tools for engaging visitors to the site and directing them to role modeling and reinforcement messages.

Information

In contrast to persuasion, information in the health care domain typically is viewed as being more neutral in tone. This view proposes that health care consumers should have access to accurate, evidence-based information as part of their treatment to help them understand it, evaluate it, make decisions about it, and monitor it. The most useful information has the following characteristics (Kemper & Metter, 2002):

- The right information (type of evidence that is needed for decision making)
- To the right person (provided to the patient or caregivers who will share in the decisions about treatment options)
- At the right time (accessible when it is needed for making decisions)
- Decision-focused (aimed at making sound decisions)
- Evidence-based (uses a balanced view of all relevant data and proof)
- Referenced (identifies authors and sources)
- Reputable (peer-reviewed or other reputable source)

- Reviewed by experts (transparency for listing writers, editors, and reviewers)
- Up-to-date (revised on a regular basis to keep pace with medical advances)
- Free from commercial bias (developed and presented objectively)
- Full disclosure (regarding who funded the information development)
- User-friendly (presented in a form and language that consumers can understand)
- Illustrated (visual and other features that help consumers understand)
- Emphasizes shared decision making (so that information can be shared with others who are helping the consumer)
- Comprehensive (fair balance of both the benefits and risks with complete disclosure available)

Meeting all of these requirements is not easy since information typically is prepared for an overall audience and not for one individual at a time. However, an awareness of (1) how persuasive (vs. informative) a prescription drug website is and (2) the extent to which a prescription drug website lacks specificity for an individual's situation would be valuable in evaluating the source of prescription drug promotion. If a prescription drug website is laden with persuasion and not providing useful information, a consumer would be wise to leave the site and find information through more reliable channels (e.g. health care professionals).

KNOWLEDGE AND RESOURCE EVALUATION (KARE)

To help summarize our suggestions, we have developed a brief self-assessment form that you could use whenever you are feeling a bit lost about how to use a prescription drug website or about how to talk with your health care professional about what you have learned from these sites. We call it the Knowledge And Resource Evaluation (KARE).

The KARE self-assessment focuses on knowing yourself (knowledge) and evaluating the prescription drug website (resource). As a self-assessment tool, it can give you insights about how you are using and reacting to the website. Also, it can give some insight about the website and what it is trying to accomplish (persuasion vs. information). Finally, your results from using this self-assessment tool could be shared with health care providers. Health care providers don't always have a lot of time to listen and when patients give them something in writing to let them know about where they are and what they need, they appreciate it and act on it.

KNOWLEDGE AND RESOURCE EVALUATION (KARE)

A Self-Assessment Tool for Interacting with Prescription Drug Websites

Know Yourself

1. What Type of Heath Care Consumer Are You?

(check the one that best describes you)

☐ **"Healthy Half"**—I have no obvious health problems and consider myself to be in excellent health. I have had little interest in health information from any source and have been largely immune to commercial messages.

☐ **"Doctor Led"**—I have lifestyle-restricting conditions and I am receptive to the messages in drug advertisements. Even though I discuss advertised medicines with my doctors, I defer to my physician's judgment and advice about what to use.

☐ **"Self-Manager"**—I have above-average health and my only complaints tend to be occasional or seasonal. I can usually self-treat with over-the-counter medications.

☐ **"Solution Seeker"**—I suffer from conditions that restrict my lifestyle and I am receptive to advertising messages. I actively seek new solutions to my health care wants and needs. I am in below-average health and sometimes take medicines to prevent symptoms rather than just treat symptoms of a disease. I read health-related publications and use the Internet to research my conditions and possible treatments. After doing my homework, I often discuss what I have learned with my physician and often ask to try a particular drug.

2. How Do You Process the Information at a Prescription Drug WebSite?

(check all that apply to you)

☐ I will spend a relatively short time at the website.
☐ I use a gut feeling for making an evaluation of the information given.
☐ I am primarily looking at the benefits of the medication.
☐ I don't have much knowledge about this medication.
☐ This website is overwhelming to me.
☐ This website makes me feel overloaded with information.

If you check more than one of these, it may be wise to leave the prescription drug website and contact your health professional for guidance.

3. How Do You Prefer to Make Decisions with Your Health Care Providers?

(check the one that best describes you)

☐ **"Paternalistic"**—I prefer that a practitioner makes the treatment decision on his or her own and then tells me about that decision using one-way communication, limited to a discussion of medical topics, with a minimum amount of information shared.

☐ **"Informed"**—I prefer one way communication from the practitioner to me that is only about medical topics. However, I want the practitioner to share all the relevant medical information with me and then let me make the treatment decision on my own.

☐ **"Shared"** I prefer two-way communication with my practitioner in which both medical and personal information is shared. After all relevant information is shared for decision making, the practitioner and I make decisions collaboratively.

Know the Source

1. Is it Persuasion?

(check all that apply)
☐ The content is filled with more benefit information than risk information.
☐ The content shows people getting relief by taking the medication.
☐ The language and visuals remind me of the product's benefits.
☐ There is content telling me what I should expect from taking the drug.
☐ There is content telling me how I can successfully take this drug.
☐ Content about benefits was easier to find than content about risks.
☐ Coupons or other incentives were part of the content.
☐ Consumer testimonials were given.

If you check more than one of these, it may be wise to leave the prescription drug website and contact your health professional for guidance.

2. Is it Information?

(check all that apply)
☐ The content contains evidence that you need for decision making.
☐ The content fits your unique situation.
☐ The content is aimed at making sound decisions about the drug.
☐ The content uses a balanced view of all relevant data and proof.

☐ Content sources are peer-reviewed or other reputable sources.
☐ The content was reviewed by experts with writers, editors, and reviewers listed.
☐ The content was free from commercial bias.
☐ The source of funding for the development of the content was identified.
☐ The content was presented in a form and language you could understand.
☐ Visual or other features aided in your understanding of the content.
☐ The content emphasized shared decision making with others.
☐ The content contained about equal amounts of benefit and risk information.
☐ Content about risks was just as easy to locate as content about benefits.
☐ Content included information about the cost of this drug in comparison with other treatments.

The more of these you checked, the more informative the prescription drug site is likely to be.

By using the KARE self-assessment, you can evaluate and use prescription drug websites for becoming more informed and for making decisions about your health care. As we bring this book to a close, we want to mention one more suggestion for helping you use prescription drug websites. There is a health care professional who is the most highly trained and knowledgeable when it comes to prescription medications and how to put all of the diversity of information about them into good decision making. That person is your pharmacist.

Know Your Pharmacist

Your pharmacist is a member of one of the most trusted and respected professions in the world. Some people already use their pharmacist as a trusted information source. However, that interaction has usually been conducted at a prescription drug counter or a small private consultation area in a pharmacy without any appointment needed. Generally, it was provided at no cost. Because the pharmacist was rarely reimbursed for these consultations, they were brief and focused mostly on the drug products that were being dispensed at that time.

Recently, however, a new service has been recognized nationally by government agencies, health insurance plans, and many employers. It is called Medication Therapy Management (MTM). It had its beginnings as part of the expansion of the U.S. Medicare program through the Medicare Modernization Act of 2003. MTM services were conceived so that therapeutic outcomes would be optimized through improved medication use and through reduced risk of adverse events (Smith & Clancy, 2006). Quickly, other government health programs and self-insured employer groups used similar approaches and also focused on improving medication therapy outcomes. There is overwhelming evidence to show that investment in MTM services can result in improved health outcomes and cost savings through reduced adverse drug events, emergency department visits, and hospitalizations (Schommer, Doucette, Johnson, & Planas, 2012). MTM is

> a distinct group of services that optimize therapeutic outcomes for individual patients. MTM services are independent of, but can occur in conjunction with, the provision of a medication product. MTM encompasses a broad range of professional activities and responsibilities within the licensed pharmacist's or other qualified health care provider's scope of practice. MTM services encompass those services being provided either via face-to-face contact or telephonically by a pharmacist or other qualified health care professional, but do not include mailings to patient. (McGivney, Meyer, Duncan-Hewitt, Hall, Goode & Smith, 2007; The Lewin Group, 2005).

When it comes to finding help with how to use a prescription drug website and make decisions about medication therapies, we propose that getting to know your pharmacist will help immensely. Since pharmacists are being reimbursed for MTM services, they have developed models of care in which they can now make appointments with patients and go over their medication therapies, including questions they may have. MTM is a relatively new health care service, so some pharmacists are a little further along in providing the service than others. If your pharmacist is not yet taking appointments for MTM, he or she likely knows of one who is and could refer you. Another option for finding a good MTM pharmacist is to contact your state pharmacy association or go to www.pharmacist.com and click on 'MTM Central'.

References

About.com Healthcare Study. (2010). (unpublished).

Action Plan for the Provision of Useful Prescription Medicine Information (1996). Steering Committee for the Collaborative Development of a Long-Range Action Plan for the Provision of Useful Prescription Medicine Information. Unpublished report submitted to The Honorable Donna E. Shalala, Secretary of the U.S. Department of Health and Human Services. Washington: DC. (December 1996). Retrieved from http://www.fda.gov/downloads/AboutFDA/CentersOffices/CDER/ReportsBudgets/UCM163793.pdf.

Adelman, R. D., Greene, M. G. & Charon, S. (1991). Issues in physician-elderly patient communication. *Ageing and Society 2*, 127–148.

Aikin, K. (2002). *Direct-to-Consumer Advertising of Prescription Drugs: Preliminary Patient Survey Results*, FDA, Division of Drug Marketing, Advertising and Communications. Rockville: MD.

Alexa (2011). www.Alexa.com. August 23, 2011.

Alexa (2013). www.Alexa.com, July 23, 2013.

American Medical Association (2011). House of Delegates Annual Meeting, *Report of the Council on Science and Public Health* 3-A-11, p. 1 www.ama-assn.org/resources/doc/csaph/a11csaph3.pdf.

Anderson, K. S. & Wasden, C. (2011). Follow-me healthcare: Patients look to health organizations that are always on. *Top Health Industry Issues of 2011, no. 6.* Retrieved from http://www.pwc.com/us/en/health-industries/publications/top-issue-06-mhealth.jhtml#.

Arazy O., Nov, O., Patterson, R., & Yeo, L. (2011). Information quality in Wikipedia: The effects of group composition and task conflict. *Journal of Management Information Systems. 2*, 71–98.

Argenti, P. & Barnes, C. M. (2009). *Digital Strategies for Powerful Corporate Communications.* New York: McGraw Hill.

Aspden, P., Wolcott, J., Bootman, J. L. & Cronenwett, L. R. (Eds.) (2006). *Preventing Medication Errors.* Washington, DC: National Academies Press.

Associated Press (2011). WebMD shares tank after 2011 forecasts lowered. Retrieved from http://news.yahoo.com/webmd-shares-tank-2011-forecasts-lowered-150009941.html.

Auton, F. (2004). The advertising of pharmaceuticals direct to consumers: a critical review of the literature and debate. *International Journal of Advertising, 23*(1), 5–52.

Barlas, S. (2008). FDA review of drug ads doesn't add up. Shortcomings concern Congress. *Pharmacy and Therapeutics, 33*, 327.

Bell, C. M., Brener, S. S., Gunraj, N., Huo, C., Bierman, A. S., Scales, D. C.,... Urbach, D. R. (2011). Association of ICU or hospital admission with unintentional discontinuation of medications for chronic diseases. *JAMA, 306*(8), 840–847.

Bell, R. A., Kravitz, R. L., & Wilkes, M. S. (1999). Direct-to-consumer prescription drug advertising and the public. *Journal of General Internal Medicine, 14*, 651–657.

Berman, A. (2004). Reducing medication errors through naming, labeling, and packaging. *Journal of Medical Systems, 28*(1), 9–29.

Bolinger, D. (1980). *Language: The loaded weapon.* New York: Longman.

Bostock, S. & Steptoe, A. (2012). Association between low functional health literacy and mortality in older adults: longitudinal cohort study. *British Medical Journal 344.* BMJ 2012;344:e1602.

Boyer, L. (2011). Which comes first, the Website or the ad? *DTC Perspectives*, March, 25–6.

Brenner, J. (2013). *Pew Internet: Social Networking*, Feb 14, 2013. Retrieved from http://www.pewinternet.org/topics/Social-Networking.aspx.

Burgess, J. & Green, J. (2009). *YouTube: Online Video and Participatory Culture.* Malden, MA: Polity Press.

Camporesi, S. (2011). Pharmacopoeia, or how many pills do we take in a lifetime? *Humanities and Health*, April 28, King's College London.

Carlson, E. H. (2011). Pharma DTC at the crossroads? 2011 Prevention DTC study results, Eye for Pharma Retrieved from, http://social.eyeforpharma.com/opinion/pharma-dtc-crossroads-2011-prevention-dtc-study-results.

Carr, N. (2008, July-August). Is Google making us stupid? *The Atlantic Monthly.* Retrieved from http://www.theatlantic.com/magazine/archive/2008/07/is-google-making-us-stupid/306868/.

Carver, K. H. (2008). A global view of the First Amendment constraints on FDA. *Food and Drug Law Journal, 63*, 151–215.

Cegedim Strategic Data (2011). Cegedim Strategic Data (CSD) ranks pharmaceutical companies' social media presence. Retrieved from http://pharmaceuticals.einnews.com/pr_news/72202109/cegedim-strategic-data-csd-ranks-pharmaceutical-companies-social-media-presence, (accessed June 30, 2013).

Centers for Disease Control and Prevention. (2011). Ambulatory care use and physician visits. Retrieved from http://www.cdc.gov/nchs/fastats/docvisit.htm.

The Chain Pharmacy Industry Profile (2001). Alexandria, VA: National Association of Chain Drug Stores.

Chelimsky, E. (1991a). *Prescription Drugs, Little is Known About the Effects of Direct-to-Consumer Advertising*. General Accounting Office, Program Evaluation and Methodology Division, 91–19. Washington, DC.

Chelimsky, E. (1991b). *Prescription Drugs, Selected Direct-to-Consumer Advertising Studies Have Methodological Flaws*. General Accounting Office, Program Evaluation and Methodology Division, 91–20. Washington, DC.

Chewning, B. A., & Sleath B. (1996). Medication decision-making and management: A client-centered model, *Social Science and Medicine, 42*, 389–398.

Choi, S. M. & Wei-Na, L. (2007). Understanding the impact of direct-to-consumer (dtc) pharmaceutical advertising on patient-physician interactions. *Journal of Advertising, 36*, 137–149.

Clauson, K. A., Polen H. H., Boulos M. N. K., & Dzenowagis J. H. (2008). Scope, completeness, and accuracy of drug information in Wikipedia. *The Annals of Pharmacotherapy, 42*, 1814–1821.

Clifford, S. (2009, April 16). FDA rules on drug ads sow confusion as applied to web. *New York Times*. Retrieved from http://www.consumerwatchdog.org/story/fda-rules-drug-ads-sow-confusion-applied-web.

Commission of the European Communities. (December 2008). Proposal for a Directive of the European Parliament and of the Council amending Directive 2001/83/EC as regards information to the general public on medicinal products subject to medical prescription, Directive 2001/83/EC on the Community code relating to medicinal products for human use. Retrieved from http://eur-lex.europa.eu/LexUriServ/LexUriServ.do?uri=COM:2008:0663:FIN:en:PDF.

Comscore (2011). Retrieved from http://www.comscore.com/Press_Events/Press_Releases/2011/5/comScore_Releases_April_2011_U.S._Online_Video_Rankings.

Consumer Health Information Corporation. (2010). Consumer Health Information Organization responds to FDA Public Hearing on patient medication information. October 4, 2010. Retrieved from http://www.prweb.com/releases/2010/10/prweb4591904.htm.

Cook, G. (1992). *The discourse of advertising*. London: Routledge, p. 32.

The Council on Ethical and Judicial Affairs of the American Medical Association. (2000). Direct-to-consumer advertisements of prescription drugs. *Food & Drug Law Journal, 55*(1), 119–24.

Cunnion, M. (2010). A time of change and opportunity. *DTC Perspectives*, 22–23.

De La Merced, M. J. (2012, June 1). Pfizer executive to take the helm of WebMD. *New York Times*. Retrieved from http://dealbook.nytimes.com/2012/06/01/pfizer-executive-to-take-the-helm-of-webmd/?_r=0.

Devgan, L., Powe, N., Blakey, B., & Makary, M. (2007). Wiki-surgery? Internal validity of Wikipedia as a medical and surgical reference, *Journal of the American College of Surgeons 205*(suppl), S76–7.

Dumitru, R. C., Burkle, T., Potapov, S., Lausen, B., Wiese, B. & Prokosch, H. U. (2007). Use and perception of internet for health related purposes in Germany: results of a national survey. *International Journal of Public Health, 52*(5), 275–85.

Dutta-Bergman, M. J. (2004). Health attitudes, health cognitions, and health behaviors among Internet health information seekers: Population-based survey. *Journal of Medical Internet Research*, 6(2), e15.

Edelman, R. (2009). Edelman trust barometer. Retrieved from http://edelmaneditions.com/2009/01/trust-barometer-2009/.

Edwards, J. (2010a). WebMD's depression test has only one (sponsored) answer: You're "at risk". BNet, February 22, 2010 Retrieved from http://www.bnet.com/blog/drug-business/web-mds-depression-test-has-only-one-sponsored-answer-youre-8220at-risk-8221/4266.

Edwards, J. (2010b). 'WebMD caves on rigged depression test—not everyone is suicidal apparently' BNet, February 26, 2010 Retrieved from http://www.bnet.com/blog/drug-business/webmd-caves-on-rigged-depression-test-not-everyone-is-suicidal-apparently/4300.

Egilman, D. & Druar, N. M. (2012). Spin your science into gold: Direct to consumer marketing within social media platforms, *Work, 41*, 4494–4502.

Elliott, C. (2010). *White coat, black hat.* Boston, MA: Beacon Press.

Engelberg Center for Health Care Reform at Brookings. (2009). Expert Workshop. *The Science of Communicating Medication Information to Consumers.* Meeting summary. New York, NY, July 21, 2009. Retrieved from http://www.brookings.edu/events/2010/0721_CMI.aspx.

Engelberg Center for Health Care Reform at Brookings. (2010). Expert Workshop. *The Science of Communicating Medication Information to Consumers.* Meeting summary. New York, NY. July 2010. Retrieved from http://www.brookings.edu/~/media/events/2010/7/21%20cmi/cmi%20expert%20workshop%20summary_20101007%20ew.pdf.

European Medicines Agency (2009). Information on benefit-risk of medicines: patients', consumers' and healthcare professionals' expectations. London. Doc ref.: EMEA/40926/2009.

Eysenbach, G. & Köhler, C. (2002). How do consumers search for and appraise health information on the world wide Web? Qualitative study using focus groups, usability tests, and in-depth interviews. *British Medical Journal, 324*, 573–7.

Farrell, J. M. (2003). The ethical implications of direct-to-consumer pharmaceutical advertising. *Philosophy and Public Policy, 23*, 20–23.

45 Federal Register 60754 (September 12, 1980).

47 Federal Register 39147 (September 7, 1982).

60 Federal Register 44182 (August 24, 1995).

66 Federal Register 15494–15495 (March 19, 2001).

75 Federal Register 23775–23777 (May 4, 2010).

Fletcher, S. W., Fletcher, R. H., Thomas D. C. & Hamann, C. (1979). Patients' understanding of prescribed drugs. *Journal of Community Health* 4(3),183–9.

Food and Drug Administration. (1997). *Guidance for Industry: Consumer-Directed Broadcast Advertisements (Draft Guidance).* Division of Drug Marketing, Advertising, and Communications (DDMAC), Rockville, MD. 62 Federal Register 43171 (July 1997).

Food and Drug Administration. (1999a). *Guidance for Industry: Consumer-Directed Broadcast Advertisements.* Division of Drug Marketing, Advertising, and Communications (DDMAC)

Rockville, MD. 64 Federal Register 43197 (July 1999). Retrieved from http://www.fda.gov/cder/guidance/index.htm.

Food and Drug Administration. (1999b). *Attitudes and Behaviors Associated with Direct-to-Consumer (DTC) Promotion of Prescription Drugs: Main Survey Results*. Office of Medical Policy, Division of Drug Marketing, Advertising and Communications. Rockville, MD.

Food and Drug Administration. (2000). *Attitudes and Behaviors Associated with Direct-to-Consumer Promotion of Prescription Drugs*, Office of Medical Policy, Division of Drug Marketing, Advertising, and Communications. Rockville, MD.

Food and Drug Administration. (2002). Center For Drug Evaluation And Research, Drug Safety And Risk Management Advisory Committee, Open Public Hearing, July 17, 2002. Gaithersburg, MD. Retrieved from http://www.fda.gov/ohrms/dockets/ac/cder02.htm.

Food and Drug Administration. (2006). *Guidance: Useful Written Consumer Medication Information* (CMI). (July 2006). Center for Drug Evaluation and Research, Center for Biologics Evaluation and Research. Rockville, MD. Retrieved from http://www.fda.gov/downloads/Drugs/GuidanceComplianceRegulatoryInformation/Guidances/ucm080602.pdf.

Food and Drug Administration (2007). DDMAC warning letter to Levulan Kerastick, April 20, 2007. Retrieved from http://www.fda.gov/Drugs/GuidanceComplianceRegulatoryInformation/EnforcementActivitiesbyFDA/default.htm.

Food and Drug Administration. (2009a). Risk Communication Advisory Committee, Minutes, February 26–27, 2009. Retrieved from http://www.fda.gov/downloads/AdvisoryCommittees/CommitteesMeetingMaterials/RiskCommunicationAdvisoryCommittee/UCM152593.pdf.

Food and Drug Administration (2009b). *Presenting Risk Information in Prescription Drug and Medical Device Promotion*. Draft Guidance. FDA, May 2009. Retrieved from http://www.reedsmith.com/library/search_library.cfm?FaArea1=CustomWidgets.content_view_1&cit_id=25050.

Food and Drug Administration (2011). DDMAC warning letter, May 5, 2011, NDA #022560/MACMIS #19629. Retrieved from http://www.fda.gov/Drugs/GuidanceCompliance-RegulatoryInformation/EnforcementActivitiesbyFDA/default.htm.

Food and Drug Administration (2012a). *Guidance for Industry: Responding to Unsolicited Requests for Off-Label Information About Prescription Drugs and Medical Devices*. Retrieved from http://www.fda.gov/downloads/drugs/guidancecomplianceregulatoryinformation/guidances/ucm285145.pdf.

Food and Drug Administration (2012b). Retrieved from http://www.fda.gov/forindustry/user-fees/prescriptiondruguserfee/default.htm.

Fox, S. (2006). *Online Health Search 2006*. Retrieved from http://www.pewinternet.org/Reports/2006/Online-Health-Search-2006.aspx.

Fox, S. (2010). Commentary: Health: Strategic Learning for Health Care. January 6, 2010. Retrieved from http://www.pewinternet.org/Commentary/2010/January/Strategic-Learning-for-Health-Care-in-2010.aspx.

Fox, S. Pew Internet and American Life Project. (2011). *The Social Life of Health Information, 2011*. Retrieved from http://www.pewinternet.org/Reports/2011/Social-Life-of-Health-Info.aspx.

Fox, S. & Duggan, M. (2013). *Health Online 2013*. Pew Internet and American Life Project. Retrieved from http://www.pewinternet.org/Reports/2013/Health-online/Summary-of-Findings.aspx.

Frosch, D. L., Grande, D., Tarn, D. M. & Kravitz, R. L. (2010). A decade of controversy: Balancing policy with evidence in the regulation of prescription drug advertising. *American Journal of Public Health, 100* (1), 24–32.

Frost, J., Okun, S., Vaughan, T., Heywood, J., & Wicks, P. (2011). Patient-reported outcomes as a source of evidence in off-label prescribing: Analysis of data from PatientsLikeMe. *Journal of Medical Internet Research, 13*(1):e6.

Gaulin, J. (2011). Social media has role in delivery of healthcare but patients should proceed with caution. *American College of Gastroenterology*. October 31, 2011. Washington DC. Retrieved from http://www.eurekalert.org/pub_releases/2011–10/acog-smh102711.php.

George, P. (2006, June). Online med sites gain patient trust. *Pharmaceutical Executive, 26*, 110–111.

Giddens, A. (1991). *Modernity and self-identity*. Cambridge: Polity Press.

Giles, J. (2005). Internet encyclopedias go head to head. *Nature, 438*, 900–901.

Glasgow, C., Schommer, J. C., Gupta, K., & Pierson, K. (2002). Promotion of prescription drugs to consumers: case study results. *Journal of Managed Care Pharmacy, 8*, 512–518.

Glinert, L. H. (1998). 'Side effect warnings in British medical package inserts: A discourse analytical approach. *International Journal of Cognitive Ergonomics, 2*(1–2), 61–74.

Glinert, L. H. (2001). Language, layout and links. *Pharmaceutical Executive, 21*, 28–30.

Glinert, L. H. (2005). TV commercials for prescription drugs: A discourse analytic perspective. *Research in Social and Administrative Pharmacy 1*, 185–210.

Glinert, L. H. (2010). Prescription drug brand Web sites: Guidance where none exists. *Innovations in Pharmacy 1*(1), 1–15.

Glinert, L. H. & Schommer, J. C. (2010). Manufacturers' prescription drug web sites: A grey area of discourse and ethics. Paper presented at the *8th Interdisciplinary Conference on Communication and Ethics*, Boston University School of Public Health, Boston, MA, June 28–30, 2010.

Global Industry Analysts, Inc. (September 2011). Report: Direct-To-Consumer (DTC) Advertising in Pharmaceuticals.

Gochman, D. S. (1997). Health behavior research, in David Gochman (ed.). *Handbook of health behavior research* (pp. 3–20). New York: Plenum Press.

Goldstein, J. (2007, August 30). Abbott Labs' in-house Wikipedia editor. *Wall St Journal*.

Goldstein, J. (2008, June 17). Drugmakers to wait on advertising new drugs. *Wall Street Journal Health Blog*. Retrieved from http://blogs.wsj.com/health/2008/06/17/drugmakers-to-wait-on-advertising-new-drugs/.

Google (2009). *A Proposal for Sponsored Links*. Google. November 2009. Retrieved from www.eyeonfda.com/files/google-fda-public-hearing-final.pdf.

Google (2010). *Five Trends in Digital Healthcare in 2010*. Google. Retrieved from http://www.slideshare.net/juanpittau/five-trends-in-digital-healthcare-in-2010.

Griffiths, K. M., Christensen, H., & Evans, K. (2002). Pharmaceutical company Websites as sources of information for consumers: How appropriate and informative are they?" *Disease Management Health Outcomes, 10,* 205–214.

Grossberg, A. (2011). Letter to New York Times Magazine, February 20, 2011, p. 6.

Hafner, K. (2007, August 19). Seeing corporate fingerprints in Wikipedia edits, *New York Times.*

Halavais, A. (2008). *Search engine society.* Malden, MA: Polity Press.

Hall, T. S. (2009). Regulating direct-to-consumer advertising with tort law: Is the law finally catching up to the market? *Western New England Law Review, 31,* 333–352.

Halliday, M. A. K. (1978). *Language as social semiotic.* Baltimore, MD: University Park Press.

Haugtvedt, C. P., & Priester, J. R. (1997). Conceptual and methodological issues in advertising effectiveness: An attitude strength perspective, in W. Wells (Ed.), *Measuring advertising effectiveness,* New York: Erlbaum.

Haugtvedt, C. P., Schumann, D. W., Schneier, W. L., & Warren, W. L. (1994). Advertising repetition and variation strategies: Implications for understanding attitude strength, *Journal of Consumer Research, 21,* 176–189.

Haugtvedt, C. P. & Wegener, D. T. (1994). Message order effects in persuasion: An attitude strength perspective, *Journal of Consumer Research, 21,* 205–218.

Haw, C. & Stubbs, J. (2011). Patient information leaflets for antidepressants: Are patients getting the information they need? *Journal of Affective Disorders, 128,* 165–70.

Healthy People 2020. (2013). Retrieved from http://www.healthypeople.gov/2020/topicsobjectives2020/.

Heffernan, V. (2011). A prescription for fear. *New York Times Magazine.* February 6, 2011. p. 14, 16.

Hesse, B. W., Nelson, D. E., Kreps, G. L., Croyle, R. T., Arora, N. K., Rimer, B. K. & Viswanath, K. (2005). Trust and sources of health information: The impact of the Internet and its implications for health care providers. Findings from the First Health Information National Trends Survey. *Archives of Internal Medicine. 165*(22), 2618–24.

Hetsroni, A, & Asya, I. (2002). A comparison of values in infomercials and commercials. *Corporate Communications, 7,* 34–45.

Hobson, K. (2011, August 15). Pharma-page Facebook commenters, Start your engines. *WSJ Health Blog.* Retrieved from http://blogs.wsj.com/health/2011/08/15/pharma-page-facebook-commenters-start-your-engines/.

Hoenig-Carlson, E. (2011). Tough demands to galvanize marketing communications. *DTC Perspectives,* March 2011, 19–21.

Holmer, A. (1999). Direct-to-consumer prescription drug advertising builds bridges between patients and physicians, *JAMA, 281,* 380.

Horne, R. & Weinman, J. (2004). The theoretical basis of concordance and issues for research, in Bond, C. (ed.) *Concordance, A partnership in medicine-taking,* London: Pharmaceutical Press.

Huh, J. & Cude, B. J. (2004). Is the information 'fair and balanced' in direct-to-consumer prescription Web sites? *Journal of Health Communication, 9,* 529–540.

Huh, J., DeLorme, D. E. & Reid, L. N. (2005). Factors affecting trust in on-line prescription drug information and impact of trust on behavior following exposure to DTC advertising. *Journal of Health Communication, 10,* 711–731.

Hymes, D. H. (1964). Introduction: Toward Ethnographies of Communication. *American Anthropologist 66* (6), 1–34.

Jackson, R., Schneider A., & Baum, N. (2011) Social media networking: YouTube and search engine optimization. *Journal of Medical Practice Management, 26,* 254–7.

Jansen, B. & Spink, A. (2006). How we are searching the world wide web. *Information. Processing and Management, 42,* 248–263.

Judd, T. S. & Kennedy, G. E. (2011). Expediency-based practice? Medical students' reliance on Google and Wikipedia for biomedical inquiries. *British Journal of Educational Technology. 42*(2), 351–360.

Kamp, J. (2003). *Pharma Marketing News,* June 2003. Retrieved from http://www.news.pharma-mkting.com/pmn26-article03.pdf, July 30, 2013.

Kaphingst, K. A. & DeJong, W. (2004). The educational potential of direct-to-consumer prescription drug advertising. *Health Affairs, 23*(4), 143–150.

Kaplan, N. (2000). Literacy beyond books. In Herman, A. & Swiss, T. (Eds.). *The World Wide Web and contemporary cultural theory* (pp. 207–234). New York, NY: Routledge.

Kaufman, D. W., Kelly, J. P., Rosenberg, L., Anderson, T. E. & Mitchell, A. A. (2002). Recent patterns of medication use in the ambulatory adult population of the United States. *JAMA, 87*(3), 337–344.

Kees, J., Fitzgerald, P. B., Kozup, J., & Scholder, P. E. (2008). Barely or fairly balancing drug risks? Content and format effects in direct-to-consumer online prescription drug promotions. *Psychology & Marketing, 25,* 675–691.

Kemper, D. W. & Metter M. (2002). *Information Therapy. Prescribed information as a reimbursable medical service.* Boise, ID.: Healthwise, Inc.

Khoo, K., Bolt, P., Babl, F. E., Jury, S. & Goldman, R. D. (2008). Health information seeking by parents in the Internet age. *Journal of Paediatrics and Child Health, 44,* 419–423.

Kimberlin, C. L. & Winterstein, A. G. (2008). *Expert and Consumer Evaluation of Consumer Medication Information.* Final report to the US Department of Health and Human Services and the Food and Drug Administration. Retrieved from www.fda.gov/downloads/AdvisoryCommittees/CommitteesMeetingMaterials/RiskCommunicationAdvisoryCommittee/UCM117149.pdf.

Kjos, A. L., Schommer, J. C. & Yuan, Y. (2010). A comparison of drug formularies and potential for cost savings. *American Health & Drug Benefits, 3*(5), 321–330.

Klein, H. A. & Isaacson, J. J. (2003). Making medical instructions usable. *Ergonomics in Design, 11,* 7–12.

Kolata, G. (1983). Prescription drug ads put FDA on the spot. *Science. 220,* 387–8.

Koppen, J. (2010). Social media and technology use among adults 50+. AARP Research, June 2010. Retrieved from www.AARP.org/socialmediasurvey.

Kubiszewski, I., Noordewier, T., & Costanza, R. (2011). Perceived credibility of Internet encyclopedias, *Computers & Education, 56,* 659–667.

Lange, P. G. (2010). Achieving creative integrity on YouTube: Reciprocities and tension, *Enculturation, 8.*

Lau, R. R. (1997). Cognitive representations of health and illness. In Gochman, D. (Ed.). *Handbook of health behavior research I,* (pp. 51–69). New York: Plenum Press.

Launder, W. (2013, December 1). FTC Examines Issues Around 'Sponsored Content'. *Wall St. Journal.*

Laurent, M. & Vickers, T. J. (2009). Seeking health information online: Does Wikipedia matter? *Journal of the American Medical Informatics Association, 16,* 471–479.

Lavsa, S. M., Corman, S. L., Culley, C. M., & Pummer, T. L. (2011). Reliability of Wikipedia as a medication information source for pharmacy students. *Currents in Pharmacy Teaching and Learning, 3,* 154–158.

Leithner, A., Maurer-Ertl, W., Glehr, M., Friesenbichler, J., Leithner, K., & Windhager, R. (2010). Wikipedia and osteosarcoma: a trustworthy patients' information? *Journal of the American Medical Information Association, 17,* 373–374.

Lemke, J. L. (2002). Travels in Hypermodality. *Visual Communication, 1,* 299–325.

Lenhart, A. (2008). *The democratization of online social networks.* Pew Internet and American Life Project. Pew Research Center. Retrieved from http://www.pewinternet.org/Presentations/2009/41--The-Democratization-of-Online-Social-Networks.aspx.

Levaggi, R., Orizio, G., Domenighini, S., Bressanelli, M., Schulz, P. J., Zani, C.,…, & Gelatti, U. (2009). Marketing and pricing strategies of online pharmacies. *Health Policy, 92,* 187–196.

Levinson, S. (1979). Activity types and language. *Linguistics, 17* (5/6), 365–399.

Levy, M. (2013). Manhattan Research, January 10, 2013. Retrieved from http://manhattanresearch.com/News-and-Events/Press-Releases/beyond-the-pill.

Levy, S. (2010, February 22). Inside The Box. *Wired.* Retrieved from http://www.wired.com/magazine/2010/02/ff_google_algorithm/.

The Lewin Group. (2005). Medication therapy management services: A critical review. *Journal of the American Pharmaceutical Association. 45,* 580–587.

Lewis, T. (2006). Seeking health information on the internet: Lifestyle choice or bad attack of cyberchondria? *Media Culture & Society, 28*(4), 521–539.

Liang, B. A. & Mackey, T. K. (2011). Prevalence and global health implications of social media in direct to consumer drug advertising. *Journal of Medical Internet Research, 13,* e64.

Liebman, M. (2001). Return on TV advertising isn't a clear picture. *Medical Marketing and Media,* November 1, 2001.

Lucassen, T. & Schraagen, J. M. (2011). Factual accuracy and trust in information: The role of expertise. *Journal of The American Society For Information Science And Technology, 62,* 1232–1242.

Lynch, P. J. & Horton, S. (1999). *Basic design principles for creating Web sites.* New Haven, CT: Yale University Press.

Macias, W. & Lewis, L. S. (2005). How well do direct-to-consumer (DTC) prescription drug Web sites meet FDA guidelines and public policy concerns? *Health Marketing Quarterly, 22,* 45–71.

Main, J. K., Argo, J. J., & Huhmann, B. A. (2004). Pharmaceutical advertising in the USA: information or influence? *International Journal of Advertising, 23*(1), 119–142.

Malloy, M. (2011). Understanding today's ePharma consumers. *DTC Perspectives*, June/July 2011, 25–26.

Malone, T., Laubacher, R., & Dellarocas, C. (2010). The collective intelligence genome. *MIT Sloan Management Review, 51*(3), 21–31.

Manhattan Research (2009). Cybercitizen Health US Survey, 2009. Retrieved from http://manhattanresearch.com/News-and-Events/Press-Releases/high-interest-little-participation-in-phr.

Manhattan Research (2011). *ePharma Consumer v10.0.* Retrieved from www.Manhattanresearch.com/epc.htm.

Manhattan Research (2012). More than half of online US adults use pharma-sponsored digital resources; Many discuss prescription drugs with a health care professional as a result. *ePharma Consumer Study*, January 25, 2012. Retrieved from http://manhattanresearch.com/News-and-Events/Press-Releases/pharma-websites-digital-resources.

Marketing Charts Staff (2009a). Search plays critical role in pharma marketing. *Marketing Charts*, August 6, 2009. Retrieved from www.marketingcharts.com/interactive/search-plays-critical-role-in-pharma-marketing-10040/.

Marketing Charts Staff (2009b). Branded sites work best for Pharma. Retrieved from http://www.marketingcharts.com/interactive/branded-sites-work-best-for-pharma-10771/.

Marketing Charts Staff. (2013a). Social networking eats up 3+ hours per day for the average American user, *Ipsos Open Thinking Exchange Survey*. Retrieved from http://www.marketingcharts.com/wp/interactive/social-networking-eats-up-3-hours-per-day-for-the-average-american-user-26049/.

Marketing Charts Staff. (2013b). 1 in 3 Americans regularly check out brands' social networking pages, *Ipsos Open Thinking Exchange Survey*. Retrieved from http://www.marketingcharts.com/wp/direct/1-in-3-americans-regularly-check-out-brands-social-networking-pages-26510/.

Martin, B. A. S., Bhimy, A. C., & Agee, T. (2002). Infomercials and advertising effectiveness: An empirical study. *Journal of Consumer Marketing, 19*, 468–480.

Mayberry, P. (2003). Testimony to *Current Status of Useful Written Prescription Drug Information for FDA*. Washington, DC: Food and Drug Administration. Open Public Hearing, July 31, 2003.

Mayer, F. S. (2003). Testimony to *Current Status of Useful Written Prescription Drug Information for FDA*. Washington, DC: Food and Drug Administration. Open Public Hearing, July 31, 2003.

Mayer, F. S. (2008). Testimony to Medical Label and Prescription Error Hearing, California Board of Pharmacy. April 12, 2008.

McEvoy, G. (2010). Patient medication information for prescription drugs. Washington, DC: Food and Drug Administration. Open Public Hearing, September 27–28, 2010.

McEvoy, G. (2012). American Society of Health-System Pharmacists (personal communication).

McGinnis, T., Strand, L. M., & Webb, C. E. (2010). *The patient-centered medical home: Integrating comprehensive medication management to optimize patient outcomes.* Washington, DC: Patient-Centered Primary Care Collaborative.

McGivney, M. S., Meyer, S. M., Duncan-Hewitt, W., Hall D. L., Goode J. R., & Smith, R. B. (2007). Medication therapy management: Its relationship to patient counseling, disease management, and pharmaceutical care. *Journal of the American Pharmaceutical Association. 47*, 620–628.

Medicines in Europe Forum. (April 2012). Patient information in Europe. Retrieved from http://english.prescrire.org/en/79/207/46296/2216/ReportDetails.aspx.

Morahan-Martin, J. M. (2004). How Internet users find, evaluate and use online health information: A cross-cultural review. *CyberPsychology and Behavior, 7*, 497–510.

Morrell, R. W., Park, D. C. & Poon, L. W. (1990). Effects of labeling techniques on memory and comprehension of prescription information in young and old adults," *Journal of Gerontology, 45*(4), 166–172.

Morris, L. A. & Pines, W. L. (2000). Regulation of pharmaceutical promotion in the twenty-first century. *Drug Information Journal, 34*, 861–873.

Morris, L., Ruffner, M. & Klimberg, R. (1987). Warning disclosures for prescription drugs. *Journal of Advertising Research, 25*(5), 25–32.

Morris, L. A., Tabak E. R. & Gondek, G. (1997). Counseling patients about prescribed medication: Twelve-year trends. *Medical Care 35*, 996–1007.

Morrow, D. G., Weiner M., Young J., Steinley D., Deer M. & Murray M. D. (2005). Improving medication knowledge among older adults with heart failure: A patient-centered approach to instruction design. *Gerontologist, 45*, 545–52.

Murray, J. (2009). Complete Abridged Guide to FDA Social Media Guidance and Regulation, *Regulationships.com*, 18 November 2009. Retrieved from http://www.regulationships.com/Blog/files/1a7612769da068dea940c8aa1074bf56-8.php.

Murray, R. K., Granner, D. K., Mays, P. A. & Rodwell, V. W. (1996). *Harper's Biochemistry*, 24th edition. Stamford, CT: Appleton & Lange.

Naik, S. & Desselle, S. P. (2007). An evaluation of cues, inducements, and readability of information on drug-specific Web sites. *Journal of Pharmaceutical Marketing & Management, 17*(3–4), 61–81.

National Assessment of Adult Literacy (NAAL), 2003. (2005). National Center for Education Statistics, US Department of Education. Retrieved from http://nces.ed.gov/naal/.

National Healthcare Quality and Disparities Reports. (2009). March 2010. Rockville, MD: Agency for Healthcare Research and Quality. Retrieved from http://www.ahrq.gov/research/findings/nhqrdr/nhqrdr09/qrdr09.html.

Nettleton S., Burrows, R. & O'Malley, L. (2005). The mundane realities of the everyday lay use of the internet for health, and their consequences for media convergence. *Sociology of Health & Illness. 27*(7), 972–992.

New Zealand Ministry of Health. (2006). *Direct-to-Consumer Advertising of Prescription Medicines in New Zealand: Summary of Submissions.* Wellington, New Zealand.

Nicholas D., Huntington P. & Williams, P. (2004). *Digital consumer health information and advisory services in the UK: A user evaluation and sourcebook.* Report submitted to the UK Department of Health. London: City University.

Nielsen, J. (1997a). *Alertbox.* October 1, 1997. http://www.useit.com/alertbox/.

Nielsen, J. (1997b). *Alertbox*. September 1, 1997. http://www.useit.com/alertbox/.

Nielsen, J. (1999). *Alertbox*. May 30, 1999. http://www.useit.com/alertbox/.

Nielsen, J. (2000). *Designing Web usability*. Indianapolis, IN: New Writers Publishing.

Nielsen, J. (2002). *Alertbox*. April 28, 2002. Retrieved from http://www.useit.com/alertbox/.

Nielsen, J. (2005a). *Alertbox*. October 3, 2005. Retrieved from http://www.useit.com/alertbox.

Nielsen, J. (2005b). *Alertbox*. March 14, 2005. Retrieved from http://www.useit.com/alertbox/.

Nielsen, J. (2006). *Alertbox*. April 17, 2006. Retrieved from http://www.useit.com/alertbox/.

Nielsen, J. (March 2007 through June 2010). *Alertbox: Current Issues in Web Usability*. Retrieved from http://www.useit.com/alertbox/.

Nielsen, J. (2008) *Alertbox*. May 6, 2008. Retrieved from http://www.useit.com/alertbox/.

Nielsen, J. (2009). *Alertbox*. April 6, 2009. Retrieved from http://www.useit.com/alertbox/.

Nielsen, J. (2010). *Alertbox*. June 3, 2010. Retrieved from http://www.useit.com/alertbox/.

Nielsen, N. (2008). Testimony before the House Energy and Commerce Committee Subcommittee on Oversight and Investigations, May 8, 2008.

Nielsen-Bohlman, L., Panzer, A. & Kindig, D. (Eds.) (2004). *Health literacy: A prescription to end confusion*. Washington, DC.: Institute of Medicine. National Academies Press.

Nordenberg, T. (January-February 1998) FDA direct to you: TV drug ads that make sense. *FDA Consumer Magazine*.

Novartis (2010). Response by Novartis, February 24, 2010, to Request for Comments Regarding Promotion of Food and Drug Administration-Regulated Medical Products Using the Internet and Social Media Tools [Docket No. FDA-2009-N-0441].

O'Leary, M. (2011). About, Dummies, and Idiots. *Information Today, 28*(3), 22–23.

Oreskovic, A. (2013, June 25). U.S. regulator tells Web search firms to label ads better. *Reuters*. Retrieved from http://www.reuters.com/article/2013/06/26/us-internet-search-idUS-BRE95P01O20130626.

Oster, K. (2002). Comments from floor. Food And Drug Administration, Center For Drug Evaluation And Research, Drug Safety And Risk Management Advisory Committee, Open Public Hearing, July 17, 2002. Gaithersburg, MD. Retrieved from http://www.fda.gov/ohrms/dockets/ac/cder02.htm.

Paasche-Orlow, M. K., Parker, R. M., Gazmararian, J. A., Nielsen-Bohlman, L. T. & Rudd, R. R. (2005). The prevalence of limited health literacy. *Journal of General Internal Medicine, 20*(2), 175–84.

Pandey, A., Patni, N., Singh, M., Sood, A., Singh, G. (2010). YouTube as a source of information on the H1N1 influenza pandemic. *American Journal of Preventive Medicine, 38*(3), e1–e3.

Pariser, E. (2011). *The filter bubble*. New York, NY: Penguin.

Patel, V. L., Branch, T. & Arocha, J. F. (2002). Errors in interpreting quantities as procedures: The case of pharmaceutical labels," *International Journal of Medical Informatics 65*(3), 193–211.

PatientsLikeMe. (2013). Retrieved from http://www.patientslikeme.com/about/user_agreement.

Payne, J. W., Bettman, J. R., & Johnson, E. J. (1993). *The adaptive decision maker*, Cambridge: Cambridge University Press.

Pearsall, B. M. & Araojo, R. (2013). FDA Studies New Strategies for Presentation of Patient Information. Therapeutic Innovation & Regulatory Science, 2168479013488881, May 10, 2013.

Peters, E., Hibbard, J., Slovic, P. & Dieckmann, N. (2007). Numeracy skill and the communication, comprehension, and use of risk-benefit information. *Health Affairs, 26*, 741–8.

Petty, R. E. & Cacioppo, J. T. (1986). *Communication and persuasion: Central and peripheral routes to attitude change*, New York: Springer-Verlag.

Pew Research Center (2012). Pew Internet & American Life Project Poll, March 31, 2012. Retrieved from http://www.pewinternet.org/.

Pharmaceutical Marketing. Ad Age insights white paper. Kantar Media. October 17, 2011. Retrieved from http://gaia.adage.com/images/bin/pdf/WPpharmmarketing_revise.pdf.

Pharmacy Times (2009). Retrieved from http://www.pharmacytimes.com/publications/issue/2010/May2010/RxFocusTopDrugs-0510.

Pharmacy Times (2010). Retrieved from http://www.pharmacytimes.com/publications/issue/2011/May2011/Top-200-Drugs-of-2010.

PharmaLive (2010a). *16th Annual DTC advertising report: Multichannel challenge*. Retrieved from www.pharmalive.com, article 9187 (accessed October 11, 2010). Newtown, PA: Canon Communication Pharmaceutical Media Group.

PharmaLive. (2010b). The true cost of social media. Retrieved from www.pharmalive.com, article 9189 (accessed October 11, 2010). Newtown, PA: Canon Communication Pharmaceutical Media Group.

Pines, W. L. (1999). A history and perspective on direct-to-consumer promotion. *Food and Drug Law Journal, 54*, 489–518.

PMLiVE (2013). Pharma's reputation declining say patient groups. Retrieved from http://www.pmlive.com/pharma_news/pharmas_reputation_declining_say_patient_groups_458739.

PM360. (April 1, 2013). The Future of Marketing. Retrieved from http://www.pm360online.com/dtc360-the-future-of-dtc-marketing/.

PricewaterhouseCoopers' Health Research Institute Survey. (September 2010). *Healthcare unwired*. Albany, NY.

Priedhorsky, R., Chen, J. Lam, S. K., Panciera, K., Terveen, L., & Riedl, J. (2007). Creating, destroying, and restoring value in wikipedia. *Proceedings of the 2007 International ACM Conference on Supporting Group Work*, New York, NY: ACM, 259–268.

Princeton Survey Research Associates. (2002). *A matter of trust: What users want from websites: a report on consumer concerns about credibility of websites*. Retrieved from http://consumersunion.org/wp-content/uploads/2013/05/a-matter-of-trust.pdf.

Public Law 104–180, Title VI, Sec 601 Effective Medication Guides, 110 Stat 1593 (1996).

Purcell, K., Brenner, J., & Rainie, L. (2012). Search engine use 2012. Pew Research Center. Pew Internet and American Life Project. Retrieved from http://www.pewinternet.org/Press-Releases/2012/Search-Engine-Use-2012.aspx.

Quantcast (2013). Retrieved from www.quantcast.com/top-sites/US, (accessed July 23, 2013).

Quintiles (2011). The new health report 2011, Quintiles. www.quintiles.com/newhealthreport.

Raynor, D. K. (2003). Consumer Medicines Information: An International Perspective. *The Chronic*Ill (Journal of Malta College of Pharmacy Practice) 7*, 7–11.

Raynor, D. K. (2008). *Consumer medicines information in Europe: Learnings from research, policy and practice*. Powerpoint presentation to the Food and Drug Administration, Washington,

DC. Retrieved from http://www.fda.gov/downloads/AdvisoryCommittees/Committees-MeetingMaterials/RiskCommunicationAdvisoryCommittee/UCM150275.pdf.

Raynor, D. K. (2013). User testing in developing patient medication information in Europe. *Research in Social and Administrative Pharmacy, 9*, 640–645.

Raynor, D. K., Svarstad B., Knapp, P., Aslani, P., Rogers, M. B, Koo, M. … Silcock, J. (2007). Consumer medication information in the United States, Europe, and Australia: A comparative evaluation. *Journal of the American Pharmacists Association. 47*, 717–724.

Reich, J. W., Erdal, K. J., & Zautra, A. J. (1997). Beliefs about control and health behaviors. In Gochman, D. (ed.). *Handbook of health behavior research I*, (pp. 93–111). New York: Plenum Press.

Reichertz, P. S. (1996). Legal issues concerning the promotion of pharmaceutical products on the internet to consumers. *Food and Drug Law Journal, 51*, 355–365.

Report to Congress. (September 2009). *Direct-to-consumer advertising's ability to communicate to subsets of the general population; Barriers to the participation of population subsets in clinical drug trials.* Food and Drug Administration Amendments Act (FDAAA) of 2007, Public Law No. 110–85 Section 901 of the Federal Food, Drug, and Cosmetic Act. Department Of Health And Human Services, Food and Drug Administration.

Ricketts, C. (2010). Google search adds medication info. *VentureBeat.com.* Retrieved from http://venturebeat.com/2010/06/22/google-health-search-adds-drug-info-upping-pharma-ad-spend/.

Rodale (2009). *Consumer reaction to DTC advertising of prescription drugs.* Prevention Magazine 12th Annual Direct to Consumer Survey. New York: Rodale. July 2009.

Rodale (2010). *Prevention Magazine releases 13th Annual DTC Survey results.* Retrieved From http://www.rodaleinc.com/newsroom/ipreventioni-magazine-releases-13th-annual-dtc-survey-results.

Rodale (2011). *Pharma DTC at the crossroads? 2011 Prevention DTC study results.* Prevention Magazine, 14th Annual Pharmaceutical Direct-to-Consumer Advertising Survey. Retrieved from http://social.eyeforpharma.com/opinion/pharma-dtc-crossroads-2011-prevention-dtc-study-results.

Rost, P. (2007). Abbott caught altering entries to Wikipedia. Retrieved from www.brandweeknrbrand.com/2007/08/abbott-caught-a.html.

Rost, K. & Roter, D. (1987). Predictors of recall of medication regimens and recommendations for lifestyle change in elderly patients. *Gerontologist, 27*(4), 510–515.

Santana, A. & Wood, D. J. (2009). Transparency and social responsibility issues for Wikipedia. *Ethics and Information Technology, 11*, 133–144.

Schapira, M. M., Nattinger, A. B. & McHorney, C. A. (2001). Frequency or probability? A qualitative study of risk communication formats used in health care. *Medical Decision Making, 21*, 459–67.

Schmitt, M. R., Miller, M. J., Harrison, D. L., Farmer, K. C., Allison, J. J., Cobaugh, D. J. & Saag, K. G. (2011). Communicating non-steroidal anti-inflammatory drug risks: Verbal counseling, written medicine information, and patients' risk awareness. *Patient Education and Counseling 83*, 391–397.

Schnarr, R. L. & Freeze, H. H. (2008). A glyconutrient sham. *Glycobiology, 18* (9), 652–657.

Schommer, J. C., Doucette, W. R., Johnson, K. A. & Planas, L. G. (2012). Positioning and integrating medication therapy management. *Journal of the American Pharmacists Association, 52*, 12–24.

Schommer, J. C., Doucette, W. R., & Worley, M. M. (2001). Processing prescription drug information under different conditions of presentation, *Patient Education and Counseling, 43*, 49–59.

Schommer, J. C., & Glinert, L. H. (2005). Television Advertisement Format and the Provision of Risk Information about Prescription Drug Products', *Research in Social and Administrative Pharmacy 1*, 185–210.

Schommer, J. C., Singh, R. L., & Hansen, R. A. (2005). Distinguishing characteristics of patients who seek more information or request a prescription in response to direct-to-consumer advertisements. *Research in Social and Administrative Pharmacy, 1*(2), 231–250.

Schondelmeyer, S. W. (2009). Recent economic trends in American pharmacy. *Pharmacy in History, 51*(3), 103–127.

Schwartz, L. M. & Woloshin, S. (2009). Lost in transmission—FDA drug information that never reaches clinicians. *New England Journal of Medicine, 361*(18), 1717.

Schwartz, L. M. & Woloshin, S. (2011) Communicating uncertainties about prescription drugs to the public: A national randomized trial. *Archives of Internal Medicine. 171*, 1463–1468.

Schwartz, L. M., Woloshin, S., Black, W. C, & Welch, H. G. (1997) The role of numeracy in understanding the benefit of screening mammography. *Annals of Internal Medicine, 127*(11), 966–972.

Seda, C. (2004). *Search engine advertising: Buying your way to the top to increase sales.* Thousand Oaks, CA: New Riders Publishing.

Senak, M. S. (2013). FDA communications, Oversight in a digital era, 2008–2013. Fleishman-Hillard International Communications. Retrieved from http://www.eyeonfda.com/eye_on_fda/2013/04/some-digital-and-social-media-guidance-fda-regulation-of-pharma-communications-in-a-digital-era-a-white-paper.html.

Senate Health Committee Analysis (2010). Retrieved from http://www.leginfo.ca.gov/pub/09-10/bill/sen/sb_1351-1400/sb_1390_cfa_20100413_163836_sen_comm.html.

Sepulveda Adams, D. (2013). Personal correspondence with Research Scientist, Dr. Daniel Sepulveda Adams, at PRIME Institute, Minneapolis, MN regarding data compiled from Med Ad News, Volumes 19–31, medadnews.com, Engel Publishing Partners, Newtown, PA.

Sheehan, K. B. (2007). Direct-to-consumer (DTC) branded drug Web sites. *Journal of Advertising, 36*, 123–135.

Shiffman, S., Gerlach, K. K., Sembower, M. A. & Rohay, J. M. (2011). Consumer understanding of prescription drug information: An illustration using an antidepressant medication. *The Annals of Pharmacotherapy, 45*, 452–458.

Shrank, W. H. & Avorn, J. (2007). Educating patients about their medications: The potential and limitations of written drug information. *Health Affairs, 26*, 731–740.

Sillence, E., Briggs, P., Harris, P. R., & Fishwick, L. (2007). How do patients evaluate and make use of online health information? *Social Science and Medicine, 64*, 1853–1862.

Smith, S. R., & Clancy, C. M. (2006). Medication therapy management programs: Forming a new cornerstone for quality and safety in Medicare. *American Journal of Medical Quality*, *21*, 276–279.

Snickars, P. & Vonderau, P. (eds.) (2009). *The YouTube reader*. Stockholm: National Library of Sweden.

Springer, P. (2009). *Ads to icons: How advertising succeeds in a multimedia age*. 2nd ed. London: Kogan Page.

Statcounter. (2013). Retrieved from http://gs.statcounter.com/#search_engine-eu-monthly-201207–201306-bar.

Sterling, G. (2010). Google adds new health-search feature for medications. *Search Engine Land*. Retrieved from http://searchengineland.com/google-adds-new-health-search-feature-for-medications-44757.

Stevenson, A., Cox, K., Britten, N., & Dundar, Y. (2004). A Systematic review of the research on communication between patients and health care professionals about medicines: The consequences for concordance," *Health Expectations, 7*, 235–245.

Strangelove, M. (2010). *Watching YouTube: extraordinary videos by ordinary people*. Toronto: University of Toronto Press.

Strecher, V. J., Champion, V. L., & Rosenstock, I. M. (1997). The health belief model and health behavior. In Gochman, D. (Ed.). *Handbook of health behavior research* I, (pp. 71–91). New York: Plenum Press.

Stremersch, S., Landsman, V. & Venkataraman, S. (2012). The relationship between DTCA, drug requests and prescriptions: Uncovering variation across specialty and space. *Marketing Science, 32*, 89–110.

Svarstad, B. L., Bultman D. C., Mount J. K. (2004). Patient counseling provided in community pharmacies: Effects of state regulation, pharmacist age, and busyness. *Journal of the American Pharmacists Association, 44*, 22–29.

Svarstad, B. L., Bultman D. C., & Tabak E. R. (2003). Evaluation of written prescription information provided in community pharmacies: a study in eight states, *Journal of the American Pharmacists Association, 43*(3), 383–393.

Tannen, D. (1979). What's in a frame? Surface evidence for underlying expectations. In Freedle, R. (Ed.) *New directions in discourse processing*, pp. 137–181. Norwood, NJ: Ablex.

Tarn, D. M., Heritage, J., Paterniti, D. A., Hays, R. D., Kravitz, R. L. & Wenger, N. S. (2006). Physician Communication When Prescribing New Medications," *Archives of Internal Medicine 166*(17), 1855–1862.

Torres, C. (2011, August 13). Drug companies lose protections on Facebook, some decide to close pages. *Washington Times*. Retrieved from http://www.washingtonpost.com/national/health-science/pharmaceutical-companies-lose-protections-on-facebook-decide-to-close-pages/2011/07/22/gIQATQGFBJ_story.html.

Udow-Phillips, M. (2011). Buyer Beware. CHRTlines, Center for Healthcare Research & Transformation, February 21, 2011. Retrieved from http://www.chrt.org/blog/buyer-beware/.

United States Supreme Court (1976). *Virginia State Pharmacy Board v. Virginia* Citizens Consumer Council, 425 U.S. 748 (1976).

URAC (2011). Retrieved from www.urac.org/consumers/resources/standards.aspx (accessed August 25, 2011).

Van Walraven, C., Jennings, A., Taljaard, M., Dhalla, I., English, S., Mulpuru, S., ... Forster, A. J. (2011). Incidence of potentially avoidable urgent readmissions and their relation to all-cause urgent readmissions. *Canadian Medical Association Journal 183*(14), E1067–72. DOI: 10.1503/cmaj.110400.

Vernon, J. A., Trujillo, A., Rosenbaum, S. & DeBuono, B. (2007). Low health literacy: Implications for national health care policy. Washington, DC: George Washington University School of Public Health and Health Services. (Center for Health Policy Research Report).

Vigilante, W. J., Jr., & Wogalter, M. S. (2005). Assessing risk and benefit communication in direct-to-consumer medication Web site advertising. *Drug Information Journal, 39*, 3–12.

Wagner, C., & Majchrzak, A. (2006–7). Enabling customer-centricity using wikis and the wiki way. *Journal of Management Information Systems, 23*(3), 17–43.

Warnick, B. (2006). Rhetoric on the Web. In Messaris, P. & Humphreys, L. (Eds.) *Digital media: Transformations in human communication.* (pp. 139–146). New York, NY: Peter Lang Publishing.

Warth, K. (2000). Is your Web site working? *Pharmaceutical Executive.* November 2000, 128–134.

Wasserstein, J. N. (2011). Social media: Why bother issuing guidance when you can issue untitled letters?, *FDA Law Blog.* May 10, 2011, http://www.fdalawblog.net/fda_law_blog_hyman_phelps/advertising-and-promotion-ddmac/.

Weiss, B. D. & Coyne, C. (1997). Communicating with patients who cannot read. *New England Journal of Medicine, 337*, 272–274.

Weissman, J. S., Blumenthal, D., Silk, A. J., Zapert, K., Newman M., Leitman R. (2003). Consumers' reports on the health effects of direct-to-consumer drug advertising. *Health Affairs*, January-June;Supplement Web Exclusives: W3–82–95.

White, H. J., Draves, L. P., Soong, R. & Moore, C. (2004). Ask your doctor! Measuring the effect of direct-to-consumer communications in the world's largest healthcare market, *International Journal of Advertising, 23*, 53–68.

Wicks, P., Massagli, M., Frost, J., Brownstein, C., Okun, S., Vaughan, T.,... Heywood J. (2010). Sharing health data for better outcomes on PatientsLikeMe. *Journal of Medical Internet Research, 12*(2):e19.

Wikipedia (2011a). *About.* Retrieved from http://en.wikipedia.org/wiki/Wikipedia:About, (accessed July 22, 2011).

Wikipedia (2011b). *Wikipedia: Recent changes patrol.* Retrieved from http://en.wikipedia.org/wiki/Wikipedia_talk:Recent_changes_patrol, (accessed July 22, 2011).

Wikipedia (2011c). *Wikipedia: Article traffic jumps.* Retrieved from http://en.wikipedia.org/wiki/Wikipedia:Article_traffic_jumps, (accessed July 18, 2011).

Wilkes, M. S., Bell, R. A. & Kravitz, R. L. (2000). Direct-to-consumer prescription drug advertising: trends, impact, and implications, *Health Affairs, 19*(2), 110–128.

Winterstein, A. G., Linden, S., Lee, A. E., Fernandez, E. M. & Kimberlin, C. L. (2010). Evaluation of consumer medication information dispensed in retail pharmacies. *Archives of Internal Medicine, 170*(15), 1317–1324.

Wokasch, M. G. (2010). *Pharmaplasia.* McFarland, WI: Wokasch Consulting.

Wolf, M. S., Davis, T. C., Tilson, H. H., Bass, P. F. III & Parker, R. M. (2006). Misunderstanding of prescription drug warning labels among patients with low literacy. *American Journal of Health-System Pharmacy 63*, June 1, 2006, 1048–1055.

Wolfe, S. M. (2002). Direct-to-consumer advertising: educational or emotional promotion? *New England Journal of Medicine, 346*, 524–525.

World Health Organization. (2003). *Adherence to long-term therapies: Evidence in action.* Geneva, Switzerland.

World Health Organization. (2013). Glossary of globalization, trade and health terms: Pharmaceutical Industry. Retrieved from http://www.who.int/trade/glossary/story073/en/index.html.

YouTube (2013). Statistics. Retrieved from http://www.youtube.com/yt/press/statistics.html (accessed July 16, 2013).

Yuan, Y. (2013). Personal correspondence with Senior Manager, Dr. Yingli Yuan at IMS Health regarding data compiled by IMS Health Integrated Promotional Services, Philadelphia, PA.

Zarcadoolas, C., Blanco, M., Boyer, J. & Pleasant, A. (2002). Unweaving the web: An exploratory study of low-literate adults' navigation skills on the world wide web. *Journal of Health Communication, 7*, 309–324.

Index

H

health insurer profit motives, 26
health literacy, 14, 35, 45–46, 140
health promotion, 8–16, 24, 139
healthcare provider organization profit
motives, 26
healthcare providers. *See* pharmacists,
physicians
healthcare reform, 26, 37
HONcode, 65–66, 73, 79, 92
Humira, 54, 57, 60–61, 124, 127

I

information, general
overload, 140, 155–156
processing, 154–155
information on health
seekers, profile of, 31, 33, 93, 117
information to consumers on
prescription drugs
commercial vendors of, 34, 137, 140
ethics of, 2–3, 135–136
evolution of, 2–6, 34
healthcare providers, counseling by,
33, 138
Internet-based
accreditation. *See also* oversight,
24, 65, 74, 107, 132–133,
145–146
actionable information, 55–56, 60,
69, 78, 132, 146
benefits to consumers, 8, 17
commercialism, 49, 133
consumer use
preference for which types of
site, 50
searching, 22–24, 29–32, 35,
51, 88
drug interactions, 124
emergency number, 55
generic equivalent, 80

information vs. promotion,
demarcation of, 9–11, 17, 22–25,
31–32, 47, 61–62, 66–67, 74, 79,
86–96, 163
language and style, 41, 45, 70–72,
79–81, 148–149, 161–164
low-literate-friendly website
design, 45
organization. *See also* World Wide
Web in general, 24, 41, 47–50,
73, 78, 80, 146–148
coherence, 24, 56, 69, 73, 79,
146–149
consumer vs. expert content,
69–70
list of contents, 41, 71–73, 127,
132, 148
navigability, 42, 47
prompt box, 78
site map, 41, 73, 132, 148
oversight, 65–74, 107, 132–133,
145–146
personalized information, 5, 140
pharmaceutical manufacturers' role,
23–26
physicians' prescribing
information, 10, 38–40, 70–72,
90, 133, 140
reliability, 65, 119, 123, 126,
139, 146
search results, 37–40
medical conditions, 14, 29,
117, 125, 140,
153–154
paid (sponsored) search results,
23, 39, 51, 62–71, 79,
106, 114
prescription drugs, 31, 37,
47, 59, 85, 90, 108–111,
125–127
side-effect warnings, 31, 55, 60,
119–121, 137–138
sourcing, 32, 39–41
sponsorship, 67–68

Gary L. Kreps, Series Editor

This series examines the powerful influences of human and mediated communication in delivering care and promoting health.

Books analyze the ways that strategic communication humanizes and increases access to quality care as well as examining the use of communication to encourage proactive health promotion. The books describe strategies for addressing major health issues, such as reducing health disparities, minimizing health risks, responding to health crises, encouraging early detection and care, facilitating informed health decisionmaking, promoting coordination within and across health teams, overcoming health literacy challenges, designing responsive health information technologies, and delivering sensitive end-of-life care.

All books in the series are grounded in broad evidence-based scholarship and are vivid, compelling, and accessible to broad audiences of scholars, students, professionals, and laypersons.

For additional information about this series or for the submission of manuscripts, please contact:

Gary L. Kreps
University Distinguished Professor and Chair, Department of Communication
Director, Center for Health and Risk Communication
George Mason University Science & Technology 2, Suite 230, MS 3D6
Fairfax, VA 22030-4444
gkreps@gmu.edu

To order other books in this series, please contact our Customer Service Department:

(800) 770-LANG (within the U.S.)
(212) 647-7706 (outside the U.S.)
(212) 647-7707 FAX

Or browse online by series:
www.peterlang.com